An antarctic fur seal asserts his dominance on a beach.

ANTARCTICA
THE LAST CONTINENT

Kim Heacox

Prepared by
The Book Division
National Geographic Society
Washington, D.C.

A pair of grey-headed albatrosses, majestic ocean birds that mate for life, preen each other on South Georgia.
PRECEDING PAGES: Chinstrap penguins gather on a rare blue iceberg in the southern Scotia Sea, near the South Sandwich Islands.

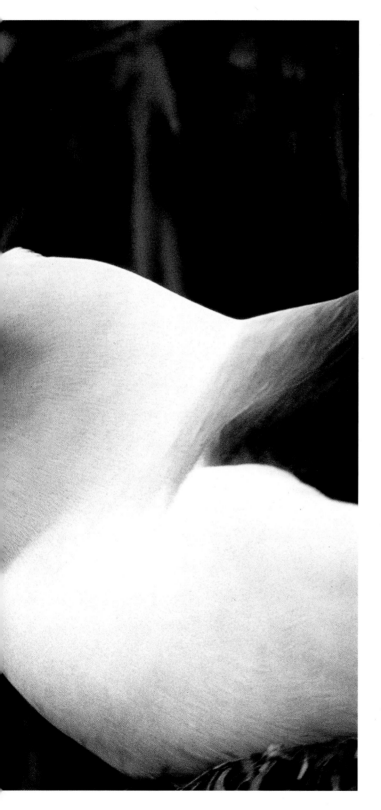

ANTARCTICA
The Last Continent

Published by
The National Geographic Society

John M. Fahey, Jr.
President and Chief Executive Officer
Gilbert M. Grosvenor
Chairman of the Board
Nina D. Hoffman
Senior Vice President

Prepared by
The Book Division

William R. Gray
Vice President and Director
Charles Kogod
Assistant Director
Barbara A. Payne
Editorial Director and Managing Editor
David Griffin
Design Director

Staff for this book
Cinda Rose
Project Editor and Art Director
Martha C. Christian
Text Editor
Greta Arnold
Illustrations Editor
Elisabeth B. Booz
Researcher
Carl Mehler
Senior Map Editor
Kristina Gibson
Map Researcher
Jehan Aziz
Map Production
Victoria A. Cooper
Contributing Editor
Janet A. Dustin
Illustrations Assistant
Peggy J. Candore, Kevin G. Craig,
Dale-Marie Herring
Staff Assistants

R. Gary Colbert
Production Director
Richard S. Wain
Production Project Manager
Lewis R. Bassford
Production

Manufacturing and Quality Control
George V. White
Director
John T. Dunn
Associate Director
Vincent P. Ryan, Gregory Storer
Managers
Polly P. Tompkins
Executive Assistant

Anne Marie Houppert
Indexer

CONTENTS

From the summit of volcanic
Mount Erebus, an adventurer
surveys the Antarctic ice and cold.

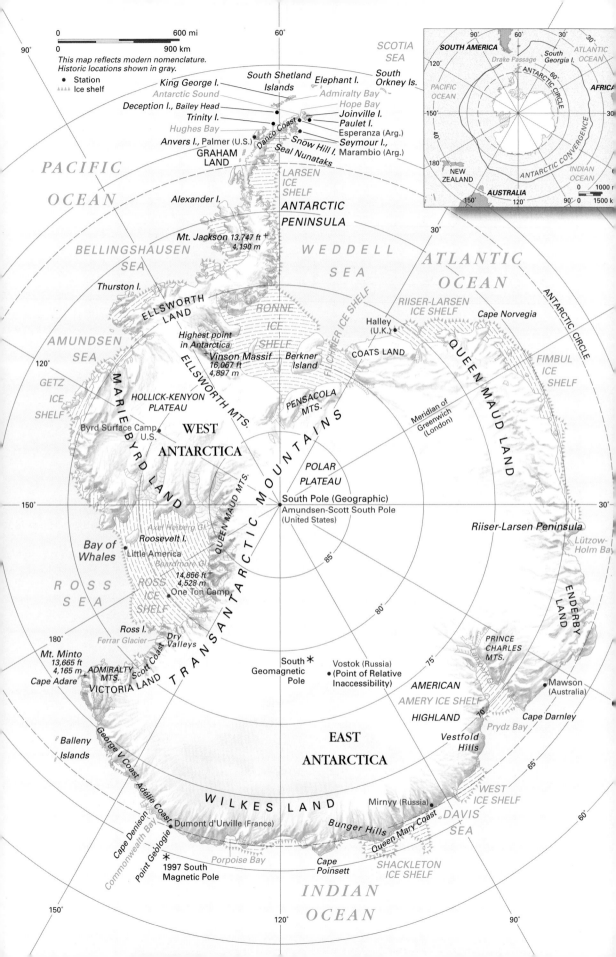

Three Antarcticas
Biological, Geopolitical, Spiritual

If any place on this precious earth belongs to everyone and to no one, it is Antarctica, the white continent. We invert the world to examine it and become inverted ourselves. We converge upon it with every line of longitude, encircle it with our high latitudes, test it with our science, and find—in turn—that it tests us. It tests not just our science but also our conscience, our poetry, our art, our arrogance, and our assumptions. It contrasts our finest technologies against a single epiphany, a simple adaptation: a seal in the sea or a mother penguin and chick on the ice who call amid a cacophony of 10,000 other penguins, their voices all the same to us, and find each other. We bow before the magic and awaken to a new beginning. It is somehow always morning here.

This coldest, windiest, driest, and highest of seven continents is at once fertile and sterile, wet and dry, inviting and inhospitable. It waits at the bottom of the world, locked in cold storage, demanding new sensibilities if we are to understand it, appreciate it, protect it. It is not empty. Rather, it is full of those things we tend to think of as emptiness: a featureless fetch of ice, a wind-tossed sea, a peopleless coast, a nameless shore. Wilderness is not a political designation here; it's an essential truth.

Terra Australis Incognita, the Unknown Southern Land, is how Egyptian geographer/cartographer Ptolemy labeled it nearly two thousand years ago. Five hundred years before him, Aristotle agreed with others that the world was round and postulated that a great landmass must exist far to the south to balance those lands in the north. Charting the northern constellation of the great bear, Arctos, the ancient Greeks reasoned that the southern sky would contain a polar complement, logically called "Anti-Arctos."

There are actually three Antarcticas. The first is biological and is defined by the Antarctic Convergence, "…perhaps the longest and most important biological barrier on Earth, as formidable as any mountain range or desert," writes biologist David G. Campbell in *The Crystal Desert.* The convergence encircles the continent and delineates a sudden and significant sea temperature gradient that arrests the dispersion of birds, fish, squid, krill, and—the most important—algae. In warmer waters north of the convergence, the sea is rich with single-celled algae called coccolithophorids; south of the convergence, diatoms. As the relative abundance of these algae species shifts, so does the population of every animal up the food chain that directly or indirectly depends upon them for food, from thumb-size krill to the largest animals on earth, blue whales. Antarctic krill, a keystone species below the convergence that feeds on diatoms, will quickly perish if dropped into warmer waters immediately to the north. And while only 36 species of birds breed below the convergence, what they lack in diversity they redeem in biomass: an estimated 70 million individuals that consume at least 7 million tons of krill and other zooplankton per year.

The second Antarctica is geopolitical. As addressed in a radical document called the Antarctic Treaty, it contains all lands and seas below latitude 60° S—roughly 10 percent of the earth's surface. First signed by 12 nations in December 1959 (and ratified in June 1961), the treaty places all territorial claims in abeyance and specifies that the continent "shall continue forever to be used exclusively for peaceful purposes." It also prohibits the deployment and detonation of nuclear devices and the disposal of nuclear waste, thus making Antarctica the world's first nuclear-free zone. Appended to this treaty—now signed by 43 nations—is a 50-year moratorium on mining. Furthermore, in May 1994 the International Whaling Commission designated all marine waters below 40° S as an 11-million-square-mile whale sanctuary.

Despite all this, however, Antarctica is not without nationalism, as 35 government-financed research stations now punctuate this once pristine world and fly their flags on a continent untouched by man a hundred years ago. Although some stations were built at the cost of evicting local residents—penguins and seals—research has brought discoveries as significant as the ozone hole, underscoring the truth that humans have created serious problems for Antarctica and must now mitigate, if not eliminate, them.

The third and perhaps most important Antarctica is spiritual. When asked why he returned there again and again to bitter cold and uncertain survival, Frank Wild, who was second-in-command of Ernest Shackleton's famed *Endurance* expedition of 1914-16, said he couldn't escape the "little voices." Like light passing through a prism, a person who goes to Antarctica is changed.

Antarctica, says writer/conservationist Bill McKibben, is "…this planet's greatest margin, its strangest edge." Most people in their workaday lives regard Antarctica as little more than an abstraction. "Protect Antarctica?" they ask. "Can't it take care of itself?" But for those who have been there and seen the fantasia of blue ice and tuxedoed birds, for those who wish to go, and for those who may never go but need to know it is there, Antarctica is a tonic.

Here we can do things right. We can pass through the prism, invert the world and ourselves, and hear little voices.

"A man doesn't begin to attain wisdom until he recognizes that he is no longer indispensable," wrote Richard Byrd, while camped alone in the Antarctic.

So, briefly humbled yet always powerful, we move into the 21st century with the fate of penguins and the earth in our hands. ∎

CHAPTER ONE

Unseen and Untrodden
Physical Geography

No student of physical geography can fully understand how the earth behaves—how it breathes, spins, freezes, and thaws on a global scale—until that student understands Antarctica and the wind-raked seas that encircle it. Living under the influence of Antarctica, as we all do to some degree, is to live in the wake of the unseen object. We influence it; it influences us. The oceans drive the atmosphere; the atmosphere drives the oceans; and Antarctica, the earth's cold engine, helps drive both. People who live and work there—mostly research scientists and support staff—whimsically call it "the ice."

That's an understatement.

Antarctica contains 90 percent of the world's ice and about 70 percent of the world's fresh surface water (locked away as ice). Stand at Wilkes Land in East Antarctica—arguably the most remote place on earth—and you stand atop 15,700 vertical feet of ice. Ice

ICICLES HANG LIKE STALACTITES from the ceiling of a crevasse inside a glacier on Adelaide Island. Not the safest place in the world, a crevasse nonetheless can offer a glimpse into the mechanics and poetry of living ice and how it shapes the earth.

so deep it descends into bedrock basins below sea level. Ice so heavy it depresses the earth's crust almost 2,000 feet; ice 10,000, 20,000, and 100,000 years old, each dark crystal and frozen lattice laced with dust particles and oxygen isotopes that speak of what the world once was, and could be again. A featureless fetch of white surrounds you. The cold bites through every layer of modern fabric. Winds knock you off your feet. December brings an insomniac sun that bathes everything in cold radiance. June closes the dark vault of the southern (austral) winter and gives new meaning to earthly notions of weather and climate. The world feels Precambrian; the air, interstellar. Only the stars and the dancing aurora australis break the indigo spell. So foreign and daunting are the physical aspects of Antarctica that you quickly realize this isn't just another place. It's another time. It's the Ice Age.

It wasn't always so. During the Jurassic period, 190 to 135 million years ago, the South Pole was cold and dark but occupied by sea, not land. Antarctica was then a core piece of a forested supercontinent called Gondwanaland, fused with Australia, India, Africa, Madagascar, and South America. A benign climate prevailed, as Gondwanaland rested at temperate and subtropical latitudes. (The name "Gondwana" comes from India where geologists first found evidence of the supercontinent's existence.) Primitive birds would one day test the world with their wings; mammals, with an even bolder experiment: giving birth to live young instead of laying eggs. But now amphibians and dinosaurs reigned, among them a small aquatic reptile, *Lystrosaurus,* two to three feet long. With nostrils and eyes on turrets atop its head, it could see and breathe when submerged.

Already preserved in the fossil record from the Permian period, 25 to 80 million years before, were the silicified remains of arborescent gymnosperms, trees 60 feet high. The growth rings of one tree, *Araucaria,* showed evidence of fire, drought, frost, and insect infestation. Another common plant was the fern *Dicroidium.* Even more ancient were marine invertebrates from half a billion years ago that would hold clues to the birth of Gondwanaland itself. All would survive tremendous sagas of travel and plate tectonics to one day emerge in fossil rocks in Antarctica, at the bottom of the world.

Midway through the Jurassic, about 150 million years ago, forces deep within the molten earth began to tear Gondwanaland asunder. The crust cracked, giving birth to volcanoes. Like geometric plates on a tortoise's carapace, the crustal pieces drifted apart, not even an inch a year, not even as fast as a fingernail grows, a slow process indeed. Yet, ceaseless and long continued, the process had dramatic effects. Africa separated first, taking Madagascar with it. Then India tore away and collided with central Asia to form the Himalaya. South America, Australia, and Antarctica remained connected for more than 50 million years, drifting as a single unit through the Cretaceous period, when flowering plants and marsupials emerged and dinosaurs peaked. The climate remained stable until 65 million years ago, when the dinosaurs abruptly disappeared—perhaps due to a cataclysmic collision of an asteroid with the earth—and mammals emerged as the dominant terrestrial life-form. South America split off from Antarctica 15 million years later, and Australia broke away relatively recently. While the others drifted east and west, the island continent of Antarctica headed south, cooling about 2°F every million years.

Life was never uninvited here; it was banished.

How perplexing it must have been to early naturalists, who knew nothing of continental drift or the creation of new species by natural selection, to find fossils of ferns in Antarctica or marine snails thousands of feet above the sea, as Charles Darwin did in the Andes of South America in the 1830s, which, among other discoveries in his seagoing youth, set him thinking on a revolutionary path. West Antarctica, which includes the long tendril of the Antarctic Peninsula, shares a recent geologic genesis with the Andes. It is a genesis of collision and subduction (one crustal plate diving below another) and the attendant volcanism, which creates new igneous rocks, and earthquakes, which lift ancient seabeds to the tops of mountains. East Antarctica on the other hand, which forms the bulk of the continent, is a broad continental shield of crystalline rock. Yet even here, in the Beacon Sandstone Series—a layer of sedimentary rock more than 8,000 feet thick in the Transantarctic Mountains, embraced now by ice and cold—fossils speak of an ancient yet unmistakable kinship to Australia, India, and other continental offspring calved from Gondwanaland.

"We found ourselves under perpendicular cliffs of Beacon sandstone, weathering rapidly and carrying veritable coal seams," wrote explorer Robert Falcon Scott in February 1912. "From the last [Edward] Wilson, with his sharp eyes, has picked several plant impressions, the last a piece of coal with beautifully traced leaves in layers, and some excellently preserved impressions of thick stems, showing cellular structure." Scott and his men had detoured to do some "geologising," as he called it. Already weak and undernourished from having trekked and hauled sledges to the South Pole and halfway back, they nonetheless found the sight of the bedrock too intoxicating to pass by—and so delayed by a dangerous margin their descent of the Beardmore Glacier onto the Ross Ice Shelf.

EVIDENCE OF A WARMER ANTARCTICA rests in the fossilized marine spiral
of an ammonite, a shelled relative of squid that became extinct millions of years
ago. Another former resident, the lobster, also remains as fossil (opposite,
below). Rocks hold minerals, too, like a copper deposit in Paradise Bay
(opposite, above). The Antarctic Treaty calls for a 50-year moratorium on mining.

EVERY CONTINENT ON EARTH—even icy Antarctica—owes part of its genesis to the power of volcanism. Deception Island (above) wears a mantle of ash over glacial ice, evidence of a volcanic eruption in 1970. Clouds boil to the rim of Mount Erebus (left) on Ross Island, the southernmost active volcano on the planet.

Wrote Scott, "A lot could be written on the delight of setting foot on rock after 14 weeks of snow and ice...."

The fossils they collected, among the youngest in Antarctica, were southern beech trees of the genus *Nothofagus* that had fringed an inland sea roughly three million years before. Antarctica had separated from its continental siblings by then but had not yet drifted south into the freezer. Cousins of those fossils, forests of *Nothofagus,* grow today around the Southern Hemisphere from New Zealand to New Guinea to Patagonia.

It made little sense before the age of modern science, without the illumination of continental drift theory, how fossils of temperate and subtropical trees, reptiles, ferns, fish, and marsupials could be found in South America, Australia, and—most perplexing—at the bottom of the world. Why this disjunct distribution? Did the marsupials swim from continent to continent? Did they ride rafts of vegetation swept out to sea? As recently as the 1970s, continental drift theory was still debunked in some scientific circles, and Antarctica's past remained a puzzle. But in 1982 paleontologists found a 40-million-year-old jawbone of a small opossum, *Polydolops,* on Seymour Island, in the northwest Weddell Sea, near the Antarctic Peninsula. Although evidence for plate tectonics was well established by then, *Polydolops* helped confirm the timing of plate movements and animal dispersal routes. Marsupials hadn't crossed from one continent to another on rafts of vegetation at sea; rather, they had walked through the ancient forests of Gondwanaland, eating berries and insects. They had rafted not on mats of vegetation, but on the continents themselves.

The drift continues. Plates subduct, mountains rise, volcanoes puff and blow, adding a sublime fire to Antarctic ice. Cinder cones lie mantled in snow. Icebergs abrade cliffs of pumice and ash. Indigo lava and olivine crystals bejewel untrodden windswept summits and rifts. The tectonic-rich Scotia Arc, including the South Orkney Islands, South Sandwich Islands, South Georgia, and Tierra del Fuego—South America's "land of fire" (and its largest island)—is composed of many small crustal plates that grind together in a ceaseless tumult of earthquakes and volcanism. One of the best anchorages in the South Shetlands, used by explorers since the 1820s, is the flooded caldera of Deception Island, a live volcano that erupted as recently as 1969 and 1970, damaging British and Chilean scientific stations so severely they had to be abandoned. The scientists left, but the chinstrap penguins did not; a breeding colony of more than 100,000 remained at Bailey Head, on the outer, windward rim of the caldera. On board the sloop *Chanticleer* in 1829, W. H. B. Webster, the ship's surgeon, described Deception Island as a "cheerless scene.... Here all is joyless and comfortless, huge masses of cinders and ashes lie strewed about, which imagination converts to the refuse of Vulcan's forge...hills of black dust and ashes topped with snow, and enormous icebergs buried beneath immense loads of volcanic matter." Webster might have been homesick or, indeed, deceived by Decep-

FOLLOWING PAGES: The approach of aircraft breaks the timeless silence high over the Queen Maud Mountains, near Scott Glacier. Most access into the interior of Antarctica is now by plane.

tion. Others have since found the caldera magical and wondrous and the nearby penguins (which Webster said "strut about with stupid mien") admirable with their white fronts, black backs, and scrappy tenacity.

When people familiar with Antarctica think of volcanoes, one mountain comes to mind: Erebus, splendid sentinel of Ross Island in McMurdo Sound. In his book, *The Worst Journey in the World,* published in 1922, Apsley Cherry-Garrard described seeing Erebus for the first time, 115 miles away. "I have seen Fuji, the most dainty and graceful of all mountains; and also Kinchinjunga: only Michel Angelo among men could have conceived such grandeur. But give me Erebus for my friend. Whoever made Erebus knew all the charm of horizontal lines, and the lines of Erebus are for the most part nearer the horizontal than the vertical. And so he is the most restful mountain in the world, and I was glad when I knew our hut would lie at his feet. And always there floated from his crater the lazy banner of his cloud of steam."

Many years later, on the summit of Erebus, Colin Monteath, a mountaineer/naturalist from New Zealand, descended by rope into the volcanic vent. As he did, he remembered an aphorism from Tom Robbins's book, *Even Cowgirls Get the Blues:* "The man who feels smug in an orderly world has never looked down a volcano." Monteath more than looked down one; after descending into the vent above a lava lake, he gained level ground and walked to a fumarole. He wrote: "…Everything seems to vibrate with the constant roar of escaping gas. Do I have a right to leave footprints on such sacred ground—to be here at all so close to the pulse of the dragon? Can this Jules Verne journey, treading a tightrope between ancient ice and heaving liquid rock, really be in the Antarctic? Fear grows with the sense of trespass. My job done, I radio to be hauled out."

If all the ice in Antarctica melted, sea level would rise 200 feet or more, and fragment the continent into many parts (and create environmental havoc around the world). The ancient bedrock shield of East Antarctica would still be a single unit, though smaller than today, while West Antarctica would split into many large islands, among them: Graham Land (the Peninsula), Ellsworth Land (the Hollick-Kenyon Plateau), Marie Byrd Land, and others. The two great seas, Ross and Weddell, would lose their ice shelves and be joined, effectively making the Transantarctic Mountains

LOOKING LIKE SPILLED MILK, the encroaching tongue of a glacier depicts ice as if it were a living organism. The behavior of glaciers such as this—how they shrink and grow—can be an important barometer for changes in global climate.

the new coast. The South Pole would be 200 miles from the sea, not 800 miles, but one can only guess how far its elevation would vary from today's 9,300 feet, perched atop its plateau of ice. The highest mountain in Antarctica, Vinson Massif at 16,067 feet in the Ellsworth Mountains, might become considerably higher when the earth's crust rebounded, freed from the crushing weight of ice. But other mountains in the world, measured against a newly raised sea level, would appear lower.

"Ice is the beginning of Antarctica and ice is its end...," wrote Stephen Pyne in *The Ice: A Journey to Antarctica.* "This is earthscape transfigured into icescape. Here is a world informed by ice: Ice that welds together a continent: ice on such a scale that it shapes and defines itself: ice that is both substance and style; ice that is both landscape and allegory." Because ice fills its interior to the brim, Antarctica is the highest continent in the world. Its average elevation is about 7,100 feet above sea level, much higher than the 2,362 feet for North America. The great ice dome that covers East Antarctica reaches heights over 13,000 feet. For millions of years ice has been accumulating here, falling heavily as snow along the coasts, collecting lightly as atmospheric ice crystals on the polar plateau. The man who drives the snowplow at the South Pole (there truly is one, at the Amundsen-Scott U.S. Research Station) doesn't attend to snow that's fallen, but rather to snow that's sculpted by fierce winds into tall drifts and sharp-edged ridges called sastrugi. Mean annual precipitation in this cold, high, crystal desert is less than two inches. The northern tip of the Antarctic Peninsula, by contrast the banana belt of Antarctica, sits at latitude 63° S (1,860 miles north of the South Pole) and receives 35 inches of annual precipitation. Annual ice accumulation in Antarctica is roughly 480 cubic miles. That same amount, perhaps slightly more due to warming temperatures in recent years, is lost by calving icebergs (discharged off ice shelves and tidewater glaciers) and by melting and evaporation. This annual gain/loss is a mere one six-thousandth of one percent of the 7,200,000 cubic miles of ice contained in the entire continent. Furthermore, a million-square-mile apron of floating sea ice surrounds Antarctica in summer, and expands to 7.3 million square miles in winter.

"As one moves from perimeter to interior, the proportion of ice relentlessly increases. Ice creates more ice, and ice defines ice," again quoting Stephen Pyne. There is fast ice and frazil ice, pack ice and pan ice, brash ice and bergy bit, grease ice and growler, ice blink and iceberg, cirque and crevasse, firn and floe, nip and nunatak. For every condition on land and sea, there is an ice; not just any ice, but an endemic ice with its own physics and behavior. Antarctica writes its signature in ice; it sculpts with ice.

Ice achieves such thickness in the interior that it buries whole mountain ranges, some with peaks up to 9,000 feet. There seems no end to it; this cup runneth over with frozen water. Yet during the Ice Age, or Pleistocene epoch, beginning two million years ago, Antarctica contained more ice than it does today. The Pleistocene was in fact many successive ice ages: as few as four, as many as ten, each perhaps 30,000 to 40,000 years long and separated by interglacial periods warmer than today. At the peak of the last Ice Age, 20,000 years ago (when continental glaciers in North America covered Canada and the northern United States down to the Ohio

ICE CARVES THE LAND; sea and sun carve the ice. Great tabular bergs calve off
ice shelves and slowly melt into fantastic shapes, such as this arched tower
near the Yalour Islands along the Antarctic Peninsula.

SUNLIGHT SHIMMERS OFF ICE near the Lonewolf Nunataks, creating an illusion of water in the cold desert of Antarctica. The blue color of the scalloped walls of an iceberg (opposite) indicates old ice. Altered by time and compression, blue ice absorbs all wavelengths of visible light except blue.

River, carved deep basins that became the Great Lakes and Puget Sound, and deposited moraines later to be called Long Island and Cape Cod), the present shoreline of Antarctica was smothered in ice. A single ice cap fused most of the South Shetland Islands. Sea level was at least 250 feet lower. The Ross, Amery, Filchner, Ronne, and Larsen Ice Shelves, now afloat, were grounded. Perhaps most striking, the Prince Charles Mountains, their summits rising about 2,600 feet above present ice levels, were buried and rounded by abrading ice.

Under tremendous pressure from its own weight, the ice of interior Antarctica splays outward—slowly, inexorably—and squeezes through perimeter mountains like toothpaste through a tube. Under the influence of gravity and geography, it then flows downslope in the form of glaciers: great ice rivers that cut and carve mountains and valleys. The largest glacier in the world, the Lambert Glacier (next to the Prince Charles Mountains), flows 250 miles through East Antarctica and empties into the Amery Ice Shelf. A veritable Amazon of ice, the Lambert is 25 miles wide and

8,200 feet deep at its junction with several tributary glaciers. More than eight cubic miles of ice pass through it each year.

Not unlike a river, a glacier expresses different rates of flow through its vertical and horizontal profiles. The fastest ice is in the center and on the surface; the slowest on the margins and the bottom, due to friction against bedrock. The bottom ice, under great pressure from the weight of ice above, exhibits a plasticity by periodically melting and refreezing as the glacier twists and turns downslope through mountainous terrain. Surface ice, by comparison, is brittle and develops crevasses that are typically a hundred feet or more in depth. But they can be deeper in extremely active glaciers.

Glaciologists refer to Antarctic glaciers as "cold" glaciers, while those in temperate regions (Canada, southeast Alaska, the Pacific Northwest, the Rocky Mountains, Chile, New Zealand, and Europe) are "warm." Summertime ice temperatures in warm glaciers are typically at or near freezing, 32°F. Meltwater forms pools on their surfaces, courses through them, and flows beneath them in large rivers. Cold, polar glaciers, by contrast, are many degrees below freezing and contain little or no meltwater.

Having descended through the mountains from the polar interior, many of the greatest of Antarctic glaciers then coalesce into massive floating ice shelves that command at least 30 percent of the continent's more than 11,000 miles of coast. The largest, the Ross Ice Shelf, is the size of France. "The barrier," early explorers called it, a fitting name for this imposing ice face that climbs 100 to 200 feet from the sea and extends for hundreds of miles. Explorers would sail along it for days, marveling how it created its own weather and rebuffed gale-driven waves. They didn't fully realize that the Ross Ice Shelf, like other Antarctic ice shelves, floats. Buttressed by bedrock shores on its margins, it buoys and undulates imperceptibly on a restless sea that reaches hundreds of miles under it. It also advances seaward half a mile a year (as does the Filchner Ice Shelf, in the Weddell Sea) and calves icebergs the size of small countries.

All ice shelves increase in thickness from their relatively thin seaward fronts, or faces, to their thick inland bases, where glaciers descend from the polar plateau and feed them new ice that compensates for what they lose in calving, melting, and evaporation. If an ice shelf or tidewater

A *DIPULMARIS* JELLYFISH DANCES on a dark, three-dimensional stage (opposite) as its kind has done for the past 20 to 30 million years. It is beautifully adapted to the cold waters of Antarctica. Starfish (above) colonize the ocean floor in McMurdo Sound.

ALGAE, THE FOUNDATION of the Antarctic food chain, grows in thick green clouds in and under seasonal sea ice (above). On South Georgia (opposite) glacial meltwater descends past moss-covered rocks.

glacier calves ice at the same rate it flows forward, as many do, its face remains in the same position, and the ice shelf, upon cursory inspection, appears motionless, static, a geographic feature as fixed and permanent as the mountains and stars. Many tidewater glaciers, unlike ice shelves, have steep profiles and tortured surfaces with deep crosshatched crevasses and tall minarets of ice, called seracs, that thunder into the sea. Ice shelves have fewer crevasses and give birth to great tabular icebergs, the largest in the world. There is seldom an icefall off an ice shelf but rather a low groan, a sharp retort, a deep *craaaaack* as a "mesa" breaks free.

"Then suddenly a racket erupted as if one hundred pieces of heavy artillery were firing in rapid succession," recalled German explorer Wilhelm Filchner in February 1912. He and his men had established base camp near the ice shelf that bears his name, deep in the Weddell Sea. From their ship, the *Deutschland,* they had unloaded supplies and dogs and ponies. They had nearly finished building a 55-by-30-foot hut, what they called a *stationhaus,* on a nearby grounded tabular iceberg when, early one morning as every man slept, chaos erupted.

First came a deep cracking, which the slumbering men didn't hear;

then explosions like cannon fire. Filchner, still on the ship, rushed topside and to his horror saw the hut with part of his crew floating north into the open Weddell Sea. Capt. Richard Vahsel reported, "All the ice in the bay is moving and the stationhaus-berg has begun to rotate." The ship itself was in danger of being crushed by huge bergs. Filchner later guessed that a sudden drop in barometric pressure and a spring tide had raised the water level 10 feet over a 230-square-mile area and had broken away more than 17 thousand billion cubic feet of ice. Over the next two days every man was rescued, and most of the stationhaus was dismantled and brought by small boat back to the ship. Only a single dog refused to be caught.

During this same time, 1911-12, on the other side of Antarctica, another explorer, Roald Amundsen, staked his fortune on the Ross Ice Shelf. A careful planner, Amundsen had pondered establishing his base camp near an indentation, called the Bay of Whales, in the ice shelf's northeastern shore. He wrote that the ice shelf "…was constantly breaking off into icebergs. The idea, therefore, of making a permanent camp on the barrier itself, though often considered, had always been dismissed as too dangerous. I had, however, carefully read and long pondered the works of the earlier explorers in the Antarctic. In comparing their records, I had been greatly struck with the discovery that the Bay of Whales, notwithstanding that it was merely a bay whose shores were the icy walls of the glacier, had not substantially changed its shore line since its first discovery by Sir James Ross in 1842. 'Surely,' I said to myself, 'if this part of the glacier has not moved in sixty-eight years, there can be only one explanation of the phenomenon—the glacier at this point must be firmly wedged on the solid rock of some great and immovable island.' The more I thought of this explanation, the more I became convinced of its truth."

Amundsen was wrong. He was also lucky. He built his base camp at the Bay of Whales without mishap. But 76 years later, in October 1987, the Ross Ice Shelf calved an iceberg 98 miles long and 22 miles wide—twice the size of Rhode Island and bearing the entire Bay of Whales. Dubbed B-9 by scientists, the iceberg contained 287 cubic miles of fresh water, enough to provide every person in the world with two glasses of drinking water per day for nearly 2,000 years. A data transponder was dropped onto it, so it could be tracked by satellite. It traveled north-northwest at two miles per day and followed a convoluted path that helped scientists understand ocean currents in the Ross Sea. In August 1989 it rammed into the Scott Coast of Victoria Land and broke into three pieces that drifted off the coast of George V Land, west of Cape Adare, one year later. The three bergs then rode the East Wind Drift nearly halfway around the continent before melting into the sea.

In the Weddell Sea, tabular bergs calve off the Filchner, Ronne, and Larsen Ice Shelves and drift northwest in the Weddell Sea Gyre—a tight, clockwise current—into Antarctic Sound, also known as "Iceberg Alley," a strait between the tip of the Antarctic Peninsula and Joinville Island. "Through the narrow Antarctic Sound they jostle, angular, flat-topped, like colossal giants on the march," wrote naturalist Mark Jones in *Wild Ice, Antarctic Journeys.* "Ponderously they ram together, abrading each other's smooth crystalline faces and reshaping the sides of small volcanic islands in their way. As far as the eye can see they crowd the horizon, many so enormous that, from the deck of the ship, it is impossible to determine where one begins and the other ends."

Sea and sun sculpt them into countless fantastic shapes: ice castles to rival Neuschwanstein and Windsor, ice arches that dwarf the arches of ancient Rome, ice buttes evocative of Monument Valley, ice inventions beyond any architect's dream or artist's palette—each a traveler riding on the backs of Antarctic seas. Some bergs, heavy with sediment excavated from mountains, reveal only 10 percent of themselves above water. Others, having tipped or rolled to expose old waterlines and ribbed erosion patterns and pewterlike surfaces, might be 15 to 20 percent exposed, depending on their ornate shapes above and below the surface. On sunny days they glisten white; on cloudy days they glow blue, as dense glacial ice absorbs every other color of the visible light spectrum.

The amount of water continually moving around Antarctica is estimated at four times greater than that of the Gulf Stream, and 400 times that of the Mississippi River. Circumpolar westerly winds (they come from the west so are called westerly) blast through stormy southern latitudes—what early mariners called the "roaring forties" and "furious fifties"—and create the West Wind Drift, a broad eastbound ocean current (pushed from west to east) that encircles the continent and isolates Antarctica from the rest of the world. This drift (also called the Antarctic Circumpolar Current) runs through the Drake Passage, which separates the southern tip of South America from the northern tip of the Antarctic Peninsula by about 600 miles, the shortest distance between mainland Antarctica and another continent. Closer to Antarctica, a narrow current flows westward, pushed by severe easterly downslope winds that descend from the cold interior and whip off the icy mainland. This nearshore East Wind Drift runs counterclockwise around Antarctica, then deflects into clockwise gyres in the embayments of the Ross, Weddell, and Bellingshausen Seas.

The strongest winds on earth have been measured at Cape Denison, on Commonwealth Bay, between Terre Adélie and the Dumont d'Urville Sea. "Home of the blizzard," Australian Douglas Mawson called it during his Australasian Antarctic Expedition of 1911-14, when he and his colleagues measured a mean annual wind speed of 45 mph, with common gusts at 140 mph, and occasional blasts to 200 mph. The mean for the windiest single day was 90 mph. Any man caught outside without crampons and a safety tether was in danger of losing his life. Quixotic winds, what the men called "whirlies," would hurl objects wildly through the air. During one storm, a 335-pound tractor case was picked up and thrown 150 feet in one direction, and an hour later picked up and thrown back. Elsewhere around Antarctica, severe localized downdrafts, called katabatic winds, can scream off glaciers and create sudden tempests, in some places actually depressing the surface of the sea with their vertical force. Then as quickly as they begin, they end, and the sea returns to relative tranquillity.

Antarctic waters move east and west, but also up and down. Vertical currents rise and dive in response to different temperatures and salinities, which affect density. As the Antarctic pack ice melts every spring, surface meltwater migrates north toward the Antarctic Convergence. This exported surface water, relatively cold and low in salinity, is replaced by imported deep water (150 to 300 feet below the surface) that travels south, upwells along the continental shelf, and forms the Antarctic Divergence: waters rich in nutrients that mix with sunlight every spring to create a robust phytoplankton bloom that is critically important to all marine life in Antarctica. Some waters from the Divergence then head north to the Convergence, where they dive to create a massive vertical gyre. Other waters head south, encounter the continental shore, and dive deep into the basement of the sea, to the ocean floor where they slide north to the Equator and beyond, a journey that takes tens or hundreds of years.

The Antarctic Convergence is not a precise line. It shifts from season to season and year to year—perhaps even from century to century. It has a higher gradient, a more abrupt change, in the South Atlantic than in the South Pacific. In 1898, as American explorer Frederick Cook sailed south across the Convergence, which was then little known or understood, he wrote: "The sudden fall of the temperature and the stinging, penetrating character of the wind seemed to warn us that ice was near; but we encountered none.... It was a night of uncertainty, of anticipation, of dis-

ON SEYMOUR ISLAND ceaseless winds sculpt snow and ice into sastrugi, sharp irregular ridges that make overland travel an ordeal in Antarctica. The ridges run parallel to the prevailing winds.

comfort—an experience which only those who have gone through the wilderness of an unknown sea can understand." Each winter as sea ice forms around Antarctica, 3 to10 feet thick and 100 to 160 miles offshore, the Convergence moves northward. And each spring it retreats back. The entire continent pulses with these physical elements—wind, water, ice, light, and darkness—that give it dimension and make it a world of extremes.

That Antarctica is the coldest continent surprises few people; the windiest, too, comes as no great shock. The title "highest continent" comes from the great bowl of ice that fills the interior to more than 13,000 feet above sea level. But the driest continent? This is unexpected until one considers that Antarctica is a freezer, and freezers aren't wet; they're dry. It's a polar icebox, a dehydrator, a crystal desert. And nowhere is the desiccating cold and timeless wind more acute than in the Dry Valleys of the Admiralty Mountains of Victoria Land, across McMurdo Sound from Ross Island, which have lain bare and arid for two million years.

The Dry Valleys were discovered by accident by Robert Falcon Scott and two companions in 1903. Low on food and fuel, the threesome, pulling sledges as the British preferred, descended the wrong glacier in thick fog. Hoping to emerge at McMurdo Sound, they instead found themselves on the edge of a frozen lake surrounded by polygonally patterned ground, in a rocky ice-free valley. Was it an apparition or an oasis? Equipped for sledging, not trekking, they had to retrace their steps. In so doing, they avoided the fate of seals and penguins that had wandered into the Dry Valleys hundreds of years ago, some of them thousands of years ago, and found it a one-way trip. Their mummified remains lie amid wind-polished rocks, offering silent testimony to entombment in the changeless dry and cold. Studying a dead Weddell Seal, Scott wrote, "…How it came to be there is beyond guessing. It certainly is a valley of the dead."

Not until 1946-47 did aerial photographic reconnaissance reveal the full extent of the Dry Valleys at more than 1,200 square miles, the largest ice-free area on the continent. Smaller dry valleys exist on the Antarctic Peninsula, in the Vestfold Hills of Princess Elizabeth Land, and in the Bunger Hills in Wilkes Land. The Bunger Hills discovery created a sensation when U.S. military personnel landed on a lake there, and the media falsely reported a lush green valley and called it a Shangri-la.

The Dry Valleys are in fact contrarian. They are not moisture in a desert, but an island of rock in a sea of ice, hardly more hospitable than their surroundings. Temperatures range from 59° to -112°F. Evaporation exceeds precipitation. Windblown sands etch and polish fine-grained rocks, called ventifacts, into three- and four-sided pyramids with intricately fluted faces. Coarse-grained rocks crumble to the ground, crystal by crystal. No animals call or cry. Nothing moves, save the wind and what it carries and a few ephemeral summertime meltwater streams that flow from glaciers. It is an erstwhile place, full of echoes. Scott noted that everywhere are "all

POWERFUL ENOUGH to knock a man off his feet, katabatic winds scream down a mountain face and over a glacier on South Georgia, lifting dust and snow into the air. These winds spring up quickly, then die with equal speed.

the indications of colossal ice action and considerable water action, and yet neither of these agents is at work now." Nor have they been for a long time. When National Aeronautics and Space Administration (NASA) scientists wanted to understand what the surface of Mars might be like and how their equipment would work there, they came to the Dry Valleys.

Unlike Mars—at least Mars as we know it—life does persist in the Dry Valleys, and in remarkably reclusive ways. Translucent, porous rocks (quartz, sandstone, some granites, and marbles) provide homes for crypto-endolithic communities of lichens, fungi, and algae that by tiny filaments and spores burrow into surface cracks and interstices between crystals (only a few millimeters deep) to survive by the thinnest of margins. Green photosynthetic cells hide deepest. The light they gather is filtered by porous rock and is thus weak, but the same rock affords protection from brutal winds. When the rock cleaves and falls to the ground, the organisms fall with it. Naked and exposed, they die. Yet a few fortuitously land on other rocks with fissures and crystal facets suitable for propagation, and a new cryptic plant community is born. Spores on the wind play even greater

WITHIN THE FREEZER OF ANTARCTICA exist several vaults called the Dry
Valleys, the largest of which are near McMurdo Sound. The Dry Valleys have
had no snow cover for two million years. Wayward seals that shuffle in seldom
get out; rather, they die and become mummified in the dry cold (opposite).
A few lakes dot the Dry Valleys but nearly all remain roofed in ice year-round.

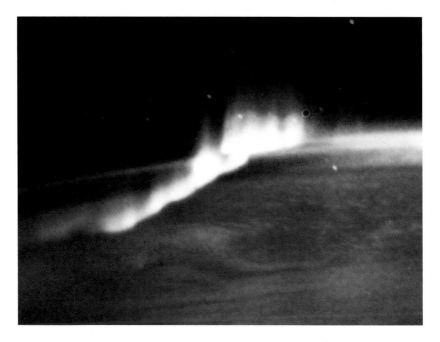

NASA SATELLITE CAPTURED this curtain of southern lights, aurora australis, as it danced through the atmosphere over Antarctica. A solar pillar (opposite) shoots skyward as the sun hides behind a horizon contoured by icebergs.

odds, as maybe one in a million alights in a rocky crevice where it becomes a pioneer and a refugee; the others, like dust, blow to oblivion.

Life in the lakes is even more bizarre. These lakes make a deceptive picture. Nearly all capped with ice, they seem abiotic and sterile. Yet beneath their permanently floating ice caps—some 10 to 12 feet thick—live aquatic mosses, green algae, and bacteria. The ice crystals align vertically and act as solar panels that capture light and transfer heat downward, a transfer so effective that the bottom waters of some lakes in the Dry Valleys are the warmest in Antarctica. They never freeze. In the dead of winter, when it's utterly dark and 60° below zero F, the waters on the bottom of Lake Vanda, 230 feet deep, can be 77°F. In summer, when sunlight floods surface ice crystals 24 hours a day, piping heat below, the waters can exceed 110°F. As the surface ice evaporates in summer, new ice forms along the ice/water margin. Dissolved salts settle to the bottom of the lake, where a brine forms that makes the bottom waters so saline and dense they cannot mix with lighter waters above. The warmest waters are not on top, but on the bottom, and are saltier than the sea.

Unlike the Arctic—which has bears, caribou, musk oxen, wolves, and foxes (what scientists call "charismatic terrestrial megafauna")—Antarctica has no land animal larger than a very coarse grain of sand. Mites,

OBLIQUE LIGHT OF MORNING catches steam rising between tendrils of ice. As cold as the sea may be, it steams because the air above it is much colder. Once ice covers the entire surface, it insulates the sea from the frigid air above.

midges, ticks, and springtails (wingless arthropods) make up the Antarctic "Serengeti." The largest terrestrial animal is an insect, a flightless midge of the genus *Belgica,* only two millimeters long.

Again unlike the Arctic, which is an ocean surrounded by continents (northern Europe, Asia, and North America), Antarctica is a continent surrounded by oceans. The Arctic has tundra and boreal forests and hundreds of species of flowering plants; Antarctica, which is only 2 percent ice-free, has no tundra, no forests, and only two species of flowering plants. Because the earth orbits the sun in an ellipse and comes closest to it in January, the South Pole receives 7 percent more radiation in the southern (austral) summer than the North Pole does in the northern summer. Yet Antarctica is much colder than the Arctic. It is higher. It is smothered in white ice and snow, which gives Antarctica an albedo of 80 percent (albedo being the amount of incoming shortwave solar radiation reflected back into space and, thus, not absorbed by the earth). By contrast, the albedo of ice-free oceans is 5 percent; of snow-free land, 15 to 35 percent. So

FOLLOWING PAGES: Birthplace of storms, great southern oceans encircle Antarctica, isolating and embracing the continent. Yet, men braved these seas to find what waited beyond.

although Antarctica is bathed in continuous light in summer, it is a cold light. What little heat arrives mostly bounces away. The coldest average temperatures have been recorded at Vostok, the Russian research station at 11,444 feet on the South Polar Plateau: -27°F in December; -91.5°F in August. The high dome of the plateau, which rises more than 13,000 feet, would measure even colder, but no research station is there. The single coldest temperature, recorded at Vostok on July 21, 1983, was -128.6°F.

Not surprisingly, no indigenous peoples live in Antarctica. They never did. There were no native hunters in sealskin boats and animal furs, no ancient spear points, no wood. A hunter in his canoe who happened into this place, like a seal into the Dry Valleys, would find it a lethal one-way trip. A Polynesian legend from the Cook Islands does tell of an adventurer, Hui-te-Rangiora, who in about A.D. 650 sailed far south of New Zealand and found a gleaming white island. An iceberg, perhaps? Historians think it unlikely he reached Antarctica itself. Others think the story, passed down from generation to generation, has been diluted or embellished by recent white men's tales from the southern oceans.

Nearly a thousand years after Hui-te-Rangiora's voyage, Sir Francis Drake, commanding five small wooden vessels under the flag of England, in 1578 sailed through waters below South America that would one day be called Drake Passage. He noted numerous animals that "...lay their eggs and bring up their young; their feeding and provision to live on is in the sea, where they swimm in such sort, as nature may seeme to have granted them no small prerogative in swiftnes...." But what exactly were the odd creatures: birds, beasts, or fish? In 1592 a Welshman called them *pen gwyn,* or "white head," thereby simply transferring to penguins the name given the similar-looking flightless great auk (now extinct) of Newfoundland.

Antarctica, little more than a dream on the charts of European cartographers and in the minds of round-earth heretics, would someday be found. When he first saw the Queen Maud Range in 1911, Norwegian explorer Roald Amundsen, a prosaic man not easily given to poetry, wrote: "Glittering white, shining blue, raven black, in the light of the sun, the land looks like a fairy tale. Pinnacle after pinnacle, peak after peak—crevassed, wild as any on our globe, it lies, unseen and untrodden."

That would change. ∎

CHAPTER TWO

Safe Return Doubtful
Exploration and Discovery

"Great God, this is an awful place...," wrote Capt. Robert Falcon Scott when he and four companions arrived on foot and ski at the South Pole in January 1912. Having relinquished their dogs, shot their ponies, man-hauled their sledges, and stumbled on skis, they were exhausted. Scott worried. Would they make it back? Could they recross the polar plateau, ski down the crevassed Beardmore Glacier through the Transantarctic Mountains, traverse the Ross Ice Shelf, and reach the coast at Cape Evans, more than 800 miles away, without starving and freezing to death?

They stood at the bottom of the world, on a great, featureless plateau of ice 9,000 feet thick and nearly that high above sea level. The temperature stood at -22°F. Thin, ominous clouds obscured the sun. A bitter wind buffeted them. The men shivered. "Now for the run home and a desperate struggle...," wrote Scott. "I wonder if we can do it."

"I WRITE OF THE FUTURE," said Robert Falcon Scott, as a young naval officer, "of the hopes of being more worthy, but shall I ever be?" Believing that an Englishman should be first to the South Pole, the often enigmatic Scott would test his ambitions on a continent as remote in some ways as himself.

In 1772, 140 years earlier, Scott's fellow Englishman, Capt. James Cook, had set sail from Plymouth, commanding two Yorkshire colliers, the *Resolution* and the *Adventure.* He carried cabbages pickled in brine; four chronometers; a crew of 190 officers, seamen, and scientists; and instructions to prove or disprove the existence of a southern polar continent. The cabbage, loaded with vitamin C, would be made into sauerkraut to prevent scurvy. The chronometers, or seagoing watches, were a new invention that would enable Cook to accurately determine longitude.

And a great southern continent? "Whether the unexplored part of the Southern Hemisphere be only an immense mass of water," Cook wrote, "or contain another continent, as speculative geography seemed to suggest, was a question which engaged the attention, not only of learned men, but most of the maritime powers of Europe."

Famous for having already mapped New Zealand and eastern Australia, Cook then sailed with the full blessings of the English elite: scientific societies, the admiralty, and even King George III, who hungered for good news and expanded empires amid his frustrations with the upstart American colonies across the Atlantic. For his efforts—commanding this first systematic scientific exploration of the southern oceans, sailing the rocky shoals and icy seas of nowhere, bringing everyone home safely and in timely fashion—Cook would be paid six shillings a day.

On January 17, 1773, the *Resolution* and the *Adventure* became the first vessels in recorded history to cross the Antarctic Circle, latitude 66° 33' S. Three weeks later a storm separated them. While the *Adventure* sailed north, the *Resolution*, with Cook in charge, pressed deep into what would someday be called the Davis Sea, south of the Indian Ocean, still one of the most remote regions on earth. Dodging pack ice and towering bergs, the small wooden ship was tossed like a toy by storms, slapped by sleet and snow, locked in the half-light of cloudy nights. "Surrounded on every side by danger," wrote Cook, "it was natural for us to wish for the daylight. This, when it came, served only to increase our apprehensions, by exhibiting to our view, those strange mountains of ice, which in the night, we had passed without seeing."

Cook retreated north, and by prior agreement reunited with the *Adventure* in New Zealand. The next season he tried again and was rebuffed by a fierce gale, which, he wrote, "froze to the Rigging as it fell, making the ropes like wires, and the sails like boards or plates of metal. The sheaves also were frozen so fast in the blocks, that it required our utmost effort to get a top-sail up and down; the cold so intense as to hardly be endured...."

Cook never did sight mainland. His misfortune was twofold. Horrible weather plagued him as he journeyed south on the tail end of a century of unseasonably cold temperatures worldwide, what scientists today call the Neoglacial period, or Little Ice Age (mid-1600s to mid-1700s), which no doubt contributed to thicker pack ice around Antarctica than exists today. And in both places where Cook pushed deepest south, at one point reaching 71° 10' S, the continental coast also turns far south.

After three years and eight days at sea, the *Resolution* arrived back in England, having traveled 60,000 miles. Cook had once again circled the southern seas and discovered many places, including South Georgia and the South Sandwich Islands. But the continent itself remained unsighted. He described the Antarctic as having an "inexpressibly horrid aspect...a country doomed by nature never once to feel the warmth of the sun's rays, but to live buried in everlasting snow and ice." He lamented uncharacteristically: "The risque one runs in exploring a coast in these unknown and icy seas, is so very great, that I can be bold enough to say that no man will ever venture farther than I have done, and the lands which may lie to the South will never be explored.... If anyone should have resolution and perseverance enough to clear up this point, by proceeding farther than I have done, I shall not envy him the honour of discovery, but I will be bold to say that the world will not be benefited by it."

Only Antarctica could prove Cook so wrong. When he died at the hands of Hawaiians in 1779, an era died with him. Europe pitched and rolled through the French Revolution and the Napoleonic Wars. England invaded a young United States in 1812. And everybody ignored the prospects of polar exploration.

Befitting its veiled and secretive nature, Antarctica was revisited in 1819 not by intention, but by accident. In February of that year Capt. William Smith, owner and master of the brigantine *Williams,* was blown far south into the Drake Passage while trying to round treacherous Cape Horn. A collier from northern England like Cook's ships 45 years earlier, the *Williams* was outfitted with additional topsails to adapt to mercurial winds and seas. Smith steered south of latitude 62° S and sighted land ten miles distant, what would become known as the South Shetland Islands, lying off the Antarctic Peninsula. He sailed to Valparaíso, Chile, and reported his discovery to a senior British naval officer who, according to one of Smith's crew, ridiculed him "for his fanciful credulity" and his preoccupation with the as yet still undiscovered southern continent.

Not to be discouraged, Smith sailed south again but was snubbed by advancing autumn storms. He retreated to Montevideo and there found

DURING CAPTAIN COOK'S third great voyage, the *Resolution* and the *Discovery* anchored at Kerguelen Island. There, crewmen found king penguins abundant and easy to kill.

a welcome audience among American sealers who mixed adventure with cutthroat business. Having already overhunted seals for their pelts—what they called "soft gold"—in Patagonia, the Falklands, South Georgia, and elsewhere, these men saw potential pay dirt in Smith's claims of unknown islands far to the south. The American sealing captains asked him: If we charter your ship, will you guide us there? A renegade who eschewed wigs to wear his black hair long and braided down his back, Smith was first and foremost an English patriot. He told the Americans no and sailed south that next spring, in October 1819, this time to land some crew on King George Island, in the South Shetlands. The men immediately planted a board marked with the Union Jack, buried a bottle of coins, and with three cheers, Smith said, "took formal possession of the new discovered land."

For better or for worse, humankind had discovered the peripheral islands of Antarctica.

FOLLOWING PAGES: In the cooling
light of a January sunset, the moon
rises over Hummock Island in
Grandidier Channel, off the Graham
Coast of the Antarctic Peninsula.

The following year no fewer than 49 sealing vessels plied the waters of the South Shetlands, most of them British and American. Years later, historian H. R. Mill wrote: "The southern summer of 1820-21 was a dark one for the fur seals whose ancestors had basked upon the shores of the South Shetlands for untold centuries, following their quaint semi-civilized life and pursuing their patriarchal customs of war and love undisturbed by any being capable of contending with them." Not anymore. The greatest alpha male seal, a Suleiman among sultans with his harem of 40 or more females, was no match for these rapacious men. Ships filled their holds with seal pelts as fast as crews could go ashore with knives and clubs and make quick work of the slaughter. The crew of one American sealer, the *Hersilia,* killed 8,868 seals that season, stopping only because they ran out of salt. The Stonington fleet took roughly 21,000. Having reoutfitted the *Williams* as a sealer and returned to the South Shetlands, Captain Smith was shocked by the mayhem he'd initiated, the wholesale slaughter and greed, the littered carcasses and bleaching bones in the cold austral air.

The Antarctic mainland was first sighted that summer and walked upon by men in sealskin boots but exactly by whom, and when, remains unknown, given incomplete journals and records. The British say the first sighting goes to their man, Edward Bransfield; the Americans say their man, Nathaniel Palmer; the Russians, their man, Thaddeus Bellingshausen. The first recorded landing, as best can be determined, belongs to the American sealing vessel *Cecilia,* under the command of Capt. John Davis, who at midday on February 7, 1821, sent a longboat ashore near Hughes Bay, on the Danco Coast. The men in that party, their names unknown, spent less than an hour onshore. They were in search of seals, not history, and probably returned to the *Cecilia* unaware of their own significance.

At midnight that same day, according to the tale later told by Nathaniel Palmer, master of the American sealing vessel *Hero,* his ship drifted in fog between Trinity Island and Deception Island when he took watch on deck and struck one bell. It brought a response. Palmer shook his head with disbelief and wrote, "I soon resumed my pace, turned my thoughts homeward and applied myself to the occupation of building castles in the air." His conclusion: No other vessel could be nearby in this netherworld of ice, rock, and sea. An hour later Palmer rang two bells "that were answered

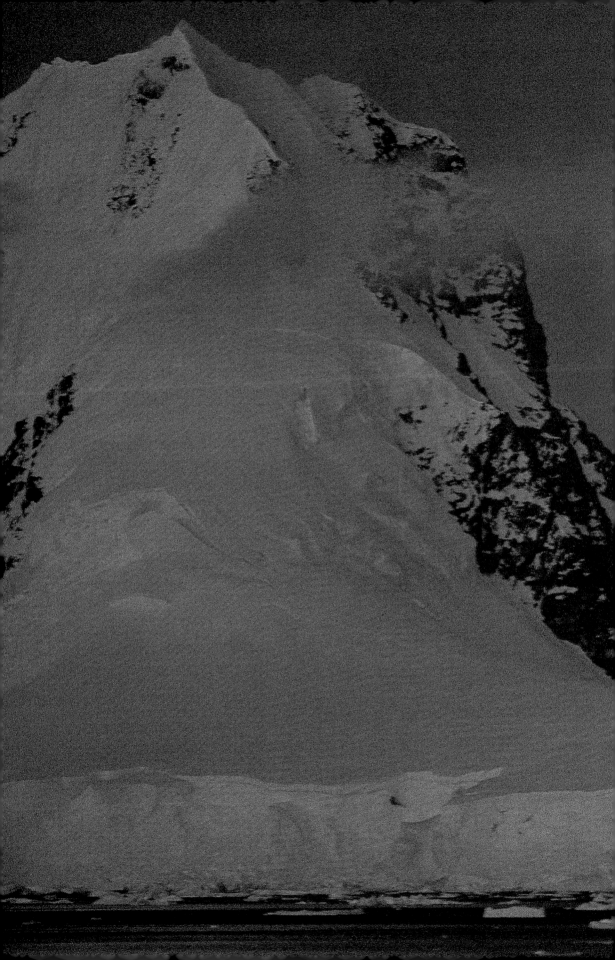

by a human hand," he wrote, "though I could not credit my ears, and I thought I was dreaming...; I was sure no living object was within leagues of the sloop." Yet hourly bells persisted, followed by human voices.

When dawn arrived and the fog lifted, Palmer was astounded to find a frigate and a sloop, the *Vostok* and the *Mirnyi,* each roughly ten times larger than the *Hero,* each flying the tsarist flag. How impressive they must have appeared: the *Vostok,* a 600-ton man-of-war with copper plating down her pinewood hull and 28 cannons, and the *Mirnyi,* fortified with tar and canvas from gunwale to keel. The combined crew of 189 officers and able-bodied seamen were each required to have two useful skills. This was no sealing venture; it was the Imperial Russian Antarctic Expedition, with Thaddeus Bellingshausen commanding.

Born in 1778, a year before Captain Cook died, Bellingshausen had studied the Englishman's methods and accomplishments and now sailed south to claim the prize Cook never did: discovery of the great southern continent. Having enrolled as a naval cadet at age 11 and graduated from a naval academy at 18, Bellingshausen served as fifth officer under A. J. von Krusenstern on the first Russian voyage around the world, from 1803 to 1806. In 1819, while stationed in the Crimea, he was called to Saint Petersburg and instructed by Tsar Alexander I to make ready two ships to sail south. Time was tight. With only six weeks to prepare for the voyage, Bellingshausen had his concerns and regrets, among them the unseasoned soft pinewood used to construct the hulls of his ships, the *Vostok* and the *Mirnyi.* Regardless, he crossed the Antarctic Circle six times in two austral summers, and his crew sighted distant mountains rising above mantles of ice and snow. Was it mainland or islands? Heavy sea ice prevented Bellingshausen from sailing farther south for verification. Uncertainty plagued him. And now an American who had emerged from the fog, full of pluck and youth, sat in his cabin aboard the *Vostok* and spoke of the many places he'd been, the things he'd seen, all in a single rambunctious season of chasing seals in Antarctica.

Though details of their meeting are incomplete, one can easily imagine the disparity between the two: Bellingshausen in full uniform, Palmer in sealer's garb; the Russian commander who would one day become an admiral, listening to an American pelt pirate only half his age.

Palmer told the Russian that 80,000 seals had been killed in Antarctica that season. Bellingshausen concluded that "there could be no doubt that round the South Shetland Islands just as at South Georgia and Macquarie Islands the number of these sea animals will rapidly decrease." Indeed. That next season, 1821-22, an estimated 320,000 seal pelts were taken from the South Shetlands alone, leaving roughly 100,000 newborn pups to starve on the beaches. By 1825, the seal trade in the far south— and the fur seal itself—was nearly extinct. Greed, ignorance, and arrogance had killed more than seals, for in neglecting moderation—the first

TEMPTING FATE IN 1842, James Clark Ross and Francis Crozier sailed the *Erebus* and the *Terror* through icebergs in the Antarctic. The ships survived but seven years later were crushed—with all hands lost—in Arctic pack ice.

rule of the successful parasite—the sealers had killed their own livelihood.

James Weddell realized this but was powerless to stop it. A merchant mariner and sealer of Scottish and English Quaker blood who rationed his crew with generous amounts of rum and good cheer, he sailed his ships *Jane* and *Beaufoy* deeper into Antarctic waters than anybody before, reaching 74° 15' S in February 1823, more than 200 miles farther south than Cook. Not until 1841 would that record be broken by James Clark Ross, who would reach 78° 10' S in his own namesake sea on the other side of Antarctica. And not until 1911 would another ship penetrate so deep into the Weddell Sea, leaving some historians to question Weddell's claims.

The "farthest south," *ne plus ultra,* became a steady preoccupation of polar explorers. Always they wondered: Who would attain it, hold it, and one day win the ultimate prize, the Pole itself? By sextant and chronometer they plotted their positions and courses, guessed their fates, and cultivated their places in history. They had no nautical charts or contour maps as we do today, no earth-synchronous satellites and global positioning systems or radar to pinpoint their positions. No telephones to call a spouse from 10,000 miles away and say a final goodbye.

UNDER CAPT. DUMONT D'URVILLE, the *Astrolabe* crossed the Antarctic Circle in January 1840. French officers and crew improvised a procession to celebrate the event (above), heralding the arrival of "Father Antarctic"— a crewman dressed comically and riding a seal. The expedition produced a 32-volume work that contained watercolors of wildlife, among them a crab, *Lithodes antarctica* (below), and a leopard seal (opposite).

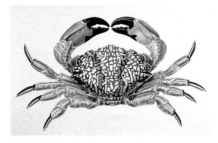

STÉNORHYNQUE AUX PETITS ONGLES. (T. Cap.)

ITS YELLOW PLUMES DANCING in the wind, the macaroni penguin (opposite) reminded explorers of an 18th-century English dandy (above), one of a class of men who dyed their hair, toured Italy, and belonged to the Macaroni Society.

Polar explorers were iron men in wooden ships who sailed on faith and moxie, driven by pride and curiosity to push the horizons of knowledge and empire. Some aspects of the high latitudes were grasped immediately, while others required more than a century to be understood. Weather and climate, for example. Just as seasons varied back home, in England, with one summer more hot and dry than another, or one winter more wet and cold, so did seasons vary in Antarctica. But here the variations were extreme, like the place itself, and this the explorers did not readily comprehend. Because James Weddell was able to sail so far south in 1823, other mariners assumed they could too. But Weddell had just happened to hit a good year when the ice pack was sparse, and those who sought to emulate him paid dearly for their assumptions.

Although Weddell saw icebergs streaked with rock and sediment, he saw no land and so assumed that an ocean occupied the South Pole. His reports created great interest back home among explorers and merchants alike. The Enderby Brothers of London, a whaling and sealing firm, sent captains south with regular dispatch for nearly four decades. The best known of these was John Biscoe, who in 1831-32 became the third mariner to circumnavigate Antarctica. Despite scurvy among his crew and fierce storms that violently tossed his two little ships—one of them, the *Tula,* was only 74 feet long—Biscoe recognized Antarctica for what it was, a large continent, not a polar sea. En route home, his second ship, the *Lively,* was wrecked in the Falklands, and his crew steadily deserted until only four men and three boys remained. Despite finding few fur seals and being a poor leader, Biscoe displayed great stamina and courage and was awarded a gold medal from the newly established Royal Geographical Society.

For nearly a century, as Antarctica and the high Arctic took shape in the map rooms in London, it was often the explorer who failed flamboyantly, rather than he who succeeded quietly, who won the greatest

prestige. England's polar heroes and tragedies would become inseparable.

Never a nation to stand by, France entered Antarctic waters in 1837 with two corvettes, the *Astrolabe* and the *Zelée*. King Louis-Philippe sought to extend his influence south by promising 100 gold francs to the crew, should they reach the 75th parallel—farther south than Weddell's 74° 15'— and an extra 20 francs for each degree of latitude beyond that. Commanding the expedition was Jules-Sébastian-César Dumont d'Urville, a lover of languages and the arts and sciences, who had circumnavigated the globe and helped secure for France the purchase of the recently unearthed statue, "Venus de Milo." Dumont d'Urville had been criticized for self-serving reports, including claims of being buffeted by 90-foot waves off the Cape of Good Hope. Antarctica would be his chance for redemption.

With their hulls sheathed in copper, the two little ships plowed south and encountered nothing like what Weddell had found 15 years before. Heavy sea ice was everywhere. At one point Dumont d'Urville followed a lead that quickly closed ahead and behind him. His expedition imprisoned by ice, he wrote: "We then had to use every means at our disposal. Men climbed down onto the ice to tie ropes to the floes.... Those who remained on board hauled on them to move painfully forward, while others tried to push the ice aside with picks, pincers and pickaxes."

After five frigid days, the ice released them into open water. But many of the crew, including all three surgeons, suffered frostbite. Scurvy followed. Dumont d'Urville retreated to Chile for the winter, where he recruited new seamen. In January 1840 during the austral summer, he crossed the Antarctic Circle—his crew showered him with rice and beans thrown from the top mast—and landed a party on the continent, or at least on an islet very near the continent. The men raised the tricolor and toasted with a bottle of Bordeaux. Dumont d'Urville named the coast for his wife, Adélie, and a species of penguin for her, also.

Soon thereafter, Dumont d'Urville's *Astrolabe,* separated from the *Zelée* in stormy weather, encountered the brig *Porpoise,* commanded by Lt. Charles Wilkes, of the United States Exploring Expedition. It was the first official overseas scientific investigation sponsored by the U.S. government, and although it was ill conceived and poorly equipped, Wilkes was bravely determined it should be a credit to his country. He explored and charted more than 1,200 miles of Antarctica's coast, establishing thereby the existence of a new continuous coastline (Wilkes Land), showing for the first time that Antarctica was a continent. Wilkes, in fact, was the first to use the term "Antarctic continent."

Three years and two months after having departed France, Dumont d'Urville returned to a hero's welcome. He had not bested Weddell's farthest south. Neither had he found the South Magnetic Pole. But for his landings, sightings, maps, and notes on the natural history and physical geography of Antarctica, he was promoted to rear admiral. His 130 surviving crewmen shared 15,000 gold francs, a gift from the king.

Late in 1840, as Dumont d'Urville and Wilkes finished their Antarctic odysseys and headed home, Capt. James Clark Ross, the most experienced of Britain's Arctic explorers of his time, left Hobart, Tasmania, where he had set up a magnetic observatory, and sailed south. Having heard news of the accomplishments of both Dumont d'Urville and Wilkes, Ross reinterpreted his orders from the British Admiralty. Rather than trace the paths of others in search of the South Magnetic Pole, he would follow a more easterly meridian.

At age 11 Ross had gone to sea, at 31 he had discovered the North Magnetic Pole on the Boothia Peninsula, in Arctic Canada. Now he would push beyond 78° S in two three-masted navy warships, the *Erebus* and the *Terror,* to discover the great sea and ice shelf that bear his name. The expedition naturalist, Joseph Dalton Hooker, only 22 when he set sail, would blossom into one of the great scientists of his time, and his collaboration with Ross would prove extremely creative and fruitful in discoveries.

Antarctica was typically quixotic: serene one day, hostile the next, always full of poetry, danger, and surprise. Sailing into his namesake sea, Ross discovered fire amid ice, a smoking volcano he named Erebus. Joseph Hooker wrote with Dickensian flourish: "This was a sight so surpassing every thing that can be imagined, and so heightened by the consciousness that we have penetrated...into regions far beyond what was ever dreamed practicable, that it really caused a feeling of awe to steal over us, at the consideration of our own comparative insignificance and helplessness....and then to see the dark cloud of smoke, tinged with flame, rising from the volcano in a perfect unbroken column; one side jet-black, the other giving back the colours of the sun, sometimes running off at a right angle by some current of wind, and stretching many miles to the leeward!"

Continuing south into waters never sailed before, Ross encountered yet another surprise, something he said "presented an extraordinary appearance, gradually increasing in height, as we got nearer to it, and proving at length to be a perpendicular cliff of ice, between one hundred and fifty and two hundred feet above the level of the sea, perfectly flat and level at the top, and without any fissures or promontories on its even seaward face." Much higher than the masts of his ships, the Victoria

Barrier—as Ross called it—was later named the Ross Ice Shelf. Of it, he wrote, "we might with equal chance of success try to sail through the cliffs of Dover, as to penetrate such a mass."

Storms threw waves onto the ships' decks and rigging, where the seawater turned to ice and had to be chipped away. Hooker was nearly crushed to death by a boat when he slipped on wet rocks during a landing. A fish was found frozen to the rail—possibly an undescribed species—and was delicately removed for inspection by the ship's surgeon. But when the surgeon turned his back, the ship's cat ate it. Perhaps the most harrowing event occurred in March 1842, when heavy seas and huge icebergs put the *Erebus* and the *Terror* in sudden peril. While reefing her topsails with a towering castle-like berg dead ahead, Ross stood on the quarterdeck of *Erebus* and watched as the *Terror*, also sailing to avoid the bergs, bore down on the *Erebus.* Collision was certain. "We instantly hove all aback to diminish the violence of the shock," wrote Ross, "but the concussion when she struck us was such as to throw almost everyone off his feet. Our bowsprit, foretopmast and other smaller spars, were carried away, and the ships hanging together, entangled by their rigging, and dashing against each other with fearful violence, were falling down upon the weather face of the lofty berg under our lee, against which the waves were breaking and foaming to near the summit of the perpendicular cliffs."

Severely crippled, the *Erebus* managed to free herself from the *Terror*, which was also damaged, only to face a gantlet of icebergs. Shouting above the shrieking winds, Ross ordered an unconventional three-point turn, a desperate maneuver in a desperate time. It took the *Erebus* nearly an hour to fill her sails and respond. "In a few minutes, after getting before the wind," Ross wrote, "she dashed through the narrow channel between two perpendicular walls of ice, and the foaming breakers which stretched across it, and the next moment we were in smooth water under its lee."

Repairs were made, and after a final Antarctic season in the Weddell Sea, Ross and his men arrived home in September 1843, seeing "Old England" for the first time in more than four years. He hadn't found the South Magnetic Pole, but he had blazed a trailhead to the South Pole—the Ross Sea and Ross Ice Shelf—and for that and great contributions to science, Queen Victoria knighted him. Later that year Ross married a woman whose

BULKY SHIPS, open boats, and tempestuous seas made whaling a dangerous occupation in the early days. That changed with the introduction of factory ships and steam-powered catcher boats with bow-mounted, cannon-fired harpoons.

father stipulated that his son-in-law forego all long polar voyages.

For 50 years, exploration declined in Antarctica, its commercial value unpromising on the ledger sheets of the industrial revolution that was sweeping Europe and the eastern United States. Sealers, however, did return to club descendants of survivors of the mass slaughter of the 1820s and made quick work of it.

Finally, in 1874, science and conservation arrived in Antarctica, when the *Challenger,* a three-masted, square-rigged corvette with auxiliary steam power, became the first steamship to cross the Antarctic Circle. A warship reoutfitted for a purely scientific expedition launched by the Royal Society, she was equipped with everything from a beam trawl for collecting specimens to a complete zoological laboratory. Her crew discovered hundreds of new marine species and founded the science of oceanography.

Less than a decade later, in 1881, the British government introduced the first regulations to control the harvest of fur seals on the Antarctic Peninsula. Commercial interests had met a challenge on the last continent.

Whalers arrived in the early 1890s in search of right whales and found none, although blue whales and other rorquals were in abundance. Capt. Carl Anton Larsen landed on Seymour Island in the Weddell Sea and

AT THE WHALING STATION Grytviken on South Georgia, all is quiet now in the harbor (right) where for more than half a century slaughtered whales were hauled onto a platform called a flensing plan (above) for processing. In 1930-31 alone more than 40,000 whales were killed in the southern oceans.

discovered petrified wood, the first fossil evidence that Antarctica was once a much warmer place, perhaps even tropical. This excited paleontologists everywhere, but Larsen managed to feel failure, for as a single-minded hunter he wanted whales; and no other discovery, regardless of its scientific significance, would compensate. The frustration worked both ways.

Sailing with another whaling expedition was a young artist, W. G. Burn Murdoch, who wrote, "And so we turned from the mystery of the Antarctic, with all its white-bound secrets still unread, as if we had stood before ancient volumes that told of the past and the beginning of all things, and had not opened them to read. Now we must go home to the world that is worn down with the feet of many people, to gnaw in our discontent the memory of what we could have done, but did not do."

Back in London in 1895, the Sixth International Geographical Congress spotlighted Antarctica with renewed vigor and called for "further explorations…before the close of the century." Several government-sponsored voyages were soon made, including that of the *Belgica,* under the command of Adrien de Gerlache, a young lieutenant in the Royal Belgian Navy. Whether he intended to or not remains debatable, but de Gerlache managed to entrap the *Belgica* and his polyglot crew in the pack ice for the long dark Antarctic winter of 1898. One crewman, a boy, had already been washed off deck during a storm and drowned. Now winter's prison slammed its door. One crewman died of a heart attack, two others lost their minds, and more would have suffered had not the ship's American physician, Frederick Cook, rallied the men with charisma, good cheer, and ingenious therapies. Cook's partner in leadership was the first mate, Roald Amundsen, a young Norwegian, not yet 30, who would soon become the greatest of all polar explorers.

The following winter, ten men under the controversial leadership of Carsten Borchgrevink, an amateur adventurer of English and Norwegian descent, settled into prefabricated huts at Cape Adare and became the first to overwinter on the Antarctic mainland. They were also the first to travel on the Ross Ice Shelf and use dogs, but Borchgrevink would have to wait 30 years for proper recognition from the English establishment, as royal societies, absorbed in petty politics, planned their own expeditions and didn't want anybody to steal their thunder.

Chief among the English Victorian elite was Sir Clements Markham, president of the Royal Geographical Society, whose principal aim was another British expedition to the Antarctic, akin to that of James Clark Ross in the 1840s, but something larger, grander—a naval expedition under naval command—using a vessel specifically built for polar exploration and science. Hearing this, an obscure young lieutenant, Robert Falcon Scott, walked across London's Buckingham Palace Road in June 1899 and rekindled an acquaintance with Sir Clements. A year later Scott, never to be obscure again, was given command of the National Antarctic Expedition.

Antarctic exploration would now graduate from the coast to the interior, as it became obvious that the South Pole and the South Magnetic Pole would have to be attained by land, not by sea, and by a special breed of men. The age of heroes was about to dawn, and Robert Falcon Scott, whether he deserved it or not, would be foremost among them. His expedition of 1901-04 was hailed a success, as scientists made important observations in magnetism, meteorology, oceanography, geology, and biology. Scott himself floated in a hot-air balloon above the Ross Ice Shelf, a first. Two parties ascended onto the polar plateau via the Ferrar Glacier, another first. But most significant, and perhaps foreshadowing, was the push for the Pole, when Scott, Edward Wilson, and Ernest Shackleton suffered snow blindness, scurvy, poor organization, and frayed nerves to reach the farthest south yet at 82° 33" S, only one-third the way to their objective.

Eighty years later, in 1983, biographer Roland Huntford would write: "Going where none has trod before, especially in the subtle Polar world, needs originality, perception, adaptability, perhaps a touch of art, none of which Scott possessed. He was vacillatory and obtuse. His Naval training had taught him form, routine, discipline, obedience, but stifled independent thought. He lacked the capacity to learn from experience.... With a lordly disregard for his technical insufficiency, he believed that British guts would see him through."

They nearly died getting back. When Shackleton openly questioned Scott's senseless decisions, Scott berated him. Never again would either man trust the other. This was 1903 after all, not 1983; a time to write history, not historical revisions, and Scott would return home a hero; "a suitable hero," Huntford wrote, "for a nation in decline."

As Scott and company staggered across the Ross Ice Shelf, fate was tempted on the other side of Antarctica as well, in the northwest Weddell Sea, where Swedish geologist Otto Nordenskjöld and five others spent two years in a 21-by-13½-foot prefabricated hut on Snow Hill Island. Nordenskjöld had intended to spend only one winter but was forced through a second when his relief ship, the *Antarctic,* commanded by Carl Larsen, was crushed in pack ice. Larsen and his crew managed to cross 25 miles of ice and sea by foot and longboat to reach tiny Paulet Island, where they survived the winter of 1903, eating penguins and seals. A third party,

FOLLOWING PAGES: More than 80 years after it was abandoned, a science lab in Robert Falcon Scott's hut at Cape Evans, on Ross Island in McMurdo Sound, speaks of dedication to detail.

SCOTT CAME TO THE POLE to research a broad array of subjects. His men launch a hot-air balloon to take atmospheric readings 820 feet above the Ross Ice Shelf. Art was a by-product: Photographer Herbert Ponting framed Scott's ship, the *Terra Nova,* from an iceberg's cavern in McMurdo Sound (opposite).

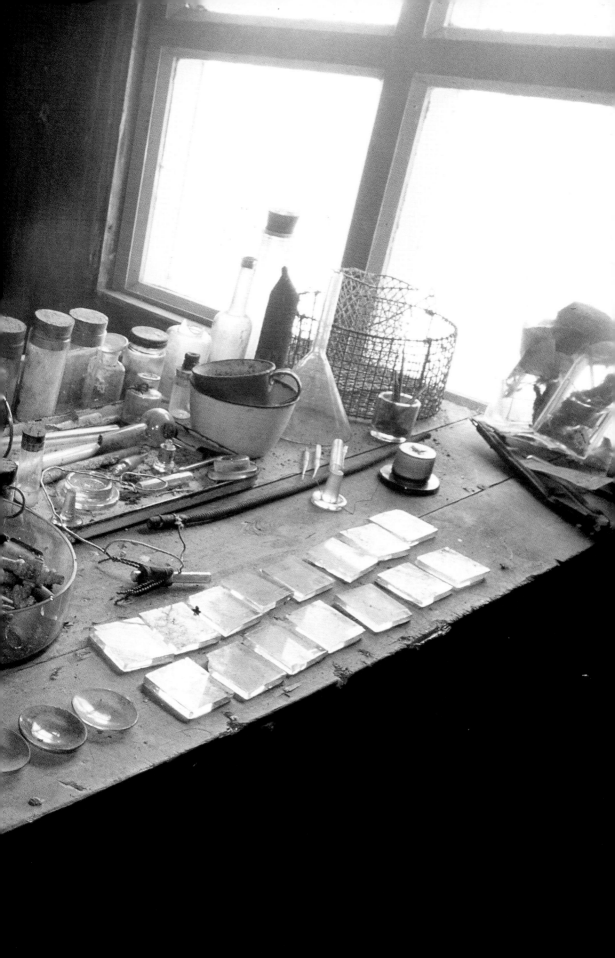

having been dropped off by Larsen at Hope Bay, at the tip of the Antarctic Peninsula, also overwintered in a makeshift hut. None of the three parties—Snow Hill, Paulet, or Hope Bay—knew the fates of the others. Amid depressing conditions, two topics commanded every discussion: food and rescue. Wrote crewman Carl Skottsberg at Paulet, "Why, we could dream through a whole dinner, from the soup to the dessert, and waken to be cruelly disappointed." Sing-alongs and readings were common, amid what Skottsberg called "hang-gallows wit." One man died. But the following spring the parties united, a rescue ship arrived, and Otto Nordenskjöld returned home with a wealth of fossils.

This was not the first expedition, nor the last, when penguins and seals served as food for men who otherwise would have perished.

At the other end of the world, a small square-sterned ship with a shallow draft and a clever captain was locked in the Arctic ice above Canada. The ship was the *Gjoa*; the captain, Roald Amundsen. From 1903 to 1906 he achieved what others had sought for 300 years: He crossed the Northwest Passage, and he did it in relative comfort, without losing a man. He believed that fewer was better, that British expeditions were too large and ponderous, and that learning from the Eskimos was more important than collecting fossils or studying magnetism. He believed that dogs, not men, should pull sledges. Men should command dogs.

Fifteen years earlier, the Norwegian Fridtjof Nansen had successfully skied across Greenland. When he returned home a hero in May 1889, sailing up Christiania Fjord amid a flotilla of boats festooned in flowers and greeting at dockside waving admirers and exuberant bands, nobody in the crowd was more impressed, or perhaps impressionable, than a 17-year-old schoolboy named Roald Amundsen. Norway was a poor country then, not yet independent, but Nansen put it on the maps and in the minds of many Europeans. Then with his revolutionary ship, the *Fram,* designed with a rounded hull to lift when squeezed by winter sea ice, Nansen drifted for three years across the Arctic Ocean, icebound, attempting to reach the North Pole. In this endeavor he failed, but in everything else he excelled, pioneering better methods of travel by dogs, sledges, and skis that would radically change polar exploration. Amundsen learned it all and then made a daring plan. Fresh from his success in the Northwest Passage, he would ask Nansen for the *Fram* and go to the North Pole.

But the world wasn't standing still. Two Americans, Frederick Cook, Amundsen's friend from the *Belgica,* and Robert Peary, each made an attempt on the North Pole, and each claimed to reach it—Cook in 1908, Peary in 1909. During this time Ernest Shackleton commanded his own expedition to Antarctica. With three companions he attempted to reach the South Pole but turned back less than a hundred nautical miles from his goal. It was a bitter disappointment, but Shackleton knew that to reach the Pole was only half the prize; the other half was to return alive. Who

THREE MEN HUDDLE IN A TENT in this drawing by Edward Wilson, Captain Scott's chief scientist and dearest friend. They were destined to die together in such a tent, trapped along with Henry "Birdie" Bowers by relentless blizzards.

could call himself a capable leader or a responsible husband, Shackleton reasoned, who reached an objective but killed himself and others doing it? He had written to his wife, Emily, "I thought you would rather have a live donkey than a dead lion."

A bulldog of a man with broad shoulders and a firm grip, Shackleton at various times had sought to dig for buried treasure, build a whaling factory, start a fleet of taxicabs, anything to circumvent a humdrum workaday life. And he was a leader who found in Antarctica what writer Alfred Lansing described as "something so enormous, so demanding, that it provided a touchstone for his monstrous ego and implacable drive. In ordinary circumstances, Shackleton's tremendous capacity for boldness and daring found almost nothing worthy of its pulling power; he was a Percheron draft horse harnessed to a child's wagon cart. But in the Antarctic—here was a burden which challenged every atom of his strength."

And it defeated him. The South Pole remained unclaimed. Yet

A 36-DAY WINTER TREK from Cape Evans to Cape Crozier in 1911 nearly
killed Scott expedition members Apsley Cherry-Garrard, right, Dr. Wilson, left,
and "Birdie" Bowers, shown here at Camp Evans after their frigid ordeal.

Shackleton's expedition did have its accomplishments, as three of his team—Edgeworth David, Alistair Mackay, and Douglas Mawson—climbed 12,448-foot Mount Erebus, a live volcano, and traveled 1,260 miles from Ross Island across Victoria Land to reach the South Magnetic Pole. Each man fell into a crevasse at least once getting there. Mawson even chipped off a piece of deep glacial ice for later study as his friends hoisted him from above. "We have pioneered a route to the magnetic pole," wrote 51-year-old David, leader of the three, "and we hope that the path thus found will prove of use to future observers."

It would not. The South Magnetic Pole, like its counterpart in the north, would drift as the earth's magnetic belts shifted and would by 1980 drift off-continent into the Dumont d'Urville Sea, precisely where the Frenchman had searched for it 140 years earlier.

When Robert Falcon Scott sailed from England in 1910 for Antarctica and the South Pole, to secure "for the British Empire the honor of that achievement," he had no idea that he was in a race. But in Melbourne, Australia, a telegram awaited him: "Beg leave to inform you, *Fram* proceeding Antarctica. Amundsen."

The clever Norwegian, who his mother once said was "the last of the Vikings," was to have sailed to the North Pole, a prize still in question as Cook and Peary each implied the other had failed. But Amundsen wanted nothing of that tangled web, so he secretly decided to sail south, not even telling his crew until after they departed Norway. While Scott established his base on Ross Island, at the edge of the Ross Ice Shelf (see map, page 160), Amundsen put his on the ice shelf itself, at the Bay of Whales, a daring plan that placed him nearly 60 miles closer to the Pole.

The winter of 1911 found both parties hunkered down in their prefabricated huts. But here again they differed. Single-minded on getting to the Pole, and getting there first, Amundsen trained himself and his men for just that task—nothing else. Scott and company, on the other hand, pursued diverse activities. One ill-fated expedition to collect emperor penguin eggs for embryology took three men—Edward Wilson, Henry "Birdie" Bowers, and Apsley Cherry-Garrard—to a nesting rookery at Cape Crozier, on the other side of Ross Island, 65 miles away. In the cold dark dead of winter they departed, pulling two sledges with 757 pounds of food and equipment. Temperatures dropped to -77°F, yet the men sweated from exertion, the perspiration turning their clothes into frozen armor. Winds shrieked around them. They found the penguins, collected the eggs, but lost their tent in a gust of wind, their only protection for the return journey. All seemed lost until Birdie Bowers found the tent caught on a rock a few hundred yards away, undamaged. As bad as it seemed, however, it got worse, as a gale hammered them deep into their sleeping bags. "Such extremity of suffering," wrote Cherry-Garrard, "cannot be measured. Madness or death may give relief. But this I know: We on this

FOLLOWING PAGES: Sled dogs like these make for efficient polar travel but have been banned from Antarctica since the mid-1990s because they carry canine distemper—a threat to seals.

journey were already beginning to think of death as a friend."

Thirty-six days after departing, the threesome staggered into base at Camp Evans, utterly exhausted, their hands and faces swollen from the cold. Their sleeping bags, which had weighed 18 pounds apiece when they departed, now weighed 45 pounds each; the difference was ice. They had succeeded. Yet in a larger sense they had failed, for during this entire time Amundsen and his men had practiced a strict regimen of sleeping, waking, and eating, saving their strength for the Pole.

On September 8, 1911, the weather broke, and Amundsen's team of 8 men and 86 dogs headed south, pulling 6 sledges. But it was a false start. A blizzard forced them to return to base after one week. Finally, on October 20 Amundsen and 4 companions, along with 52 dogs and 4 sledges, began their dash to the South Pole.

Scott's polar expedition didn't begin until November 1, already 200 miles behind Amundsen. And while the Norwegians traveled light and fast, Scott commanded a Byzantine caravan of 16 men, 10 Siberian ponies, 233 dogs, and 13 motor sledges. Unwilling to trust any one method of travel, he'd brought them all. Both expeditions had established food depots previously along their routes. In one stretch of equal length, Scott had put in two depots, Amundsen seven. And while Scott's men hauled sledges and averaged 9.8 miles a day, Amundsen's men skied—the dogs hauled the sledges—and averaged 13.3 miles a day.

After crossing the Ross Ice Shelf, the Norwegians ascended the Axel Heiberg Glacier onto the polar plateau, from 500 feet to 10,000 feet elevation in five days, and negotiated icefalls and crevasses with clinical precision. They crossed the polar plateau, with champion Nordic skier Olav Bjaaland kicking and gliding in the lead, and reached the South Pole on December 14, 1911. They shook hands, erected flags and a tent, and fixed their position. "God be thanked!" wrote Amundsen.

Three hundred and sixty miles away, Scott struggled up the Beardmore Glacier. At the top, he added an unplanned fifth man, Birdie Bowers, from the support party to the polar party, without adding rations. Pressing on, he approached his prize on January 17, 1912, five weeks after Amundsen's triumph, only to see the black flags fluttering.

His spirits ebbed. "The Pole," he wrote bitterly, "...but under very

AT COMMONWEALTH BAY, the windiest place in Antarctica, two men in a blizzard chop ice for water in a 1912 photograph by Frank Hurley. The weather-beaten hut, built by Douglas Mawson and other Australians, still stands today.

different circumstances from those expected.... Terrible enough to have laboured to it without the reward of priority."

Weakened by low morale, light frostbite, and early scurvy, the five Englishmen began the long trek home. Harnessed to their sledges like mules, every day they burned more calories than they consumed—a recipe for disaster in polar extremes. "Finding each new [food] depot now became a crisis," wrote Roland Huntford, "because there were none of Amundsen's ingenious transverse markings, but merely a single, inadequate flag. Cairnes were too low, badly made, and too few for navigation."

Descending the crevassed Beardmore Glacier, with two men seriously ill, Scott detoured to collect 30 pounds of fossils, then got lost. Ten days later, on February 18, Edgar Evans died. On the Ross Ice Shelf, Scott fought off starvation and the deepening cold, barely reaching one food depot after another. It was march or die, with no margin for error. Eleven miles south of One Ton Camp, the largest food depot, a fierce blizzard pinned them down. On his 32nd birthday Titus Oates, his feet ruined with frostbite, said to Scott in the tent, "I am just going outside and may be some time." He was never seen again.

The storm howled and refused to abate. As his life ebbed away, Scott wrote, "We are showing that Englishmen can still die with a bold spirit, fighting it out to the end...."

And to his mother, Bowers wrote, "Oh, how I do feel for you when you hear all, you will know that for me the end was peaceful as it is only sleep in the cold."

Amundsen and his men sailed from Antarctica and cabled news of their success a full three weeks before Scott, Wilson, and Bowers froze to death on the Ross Ice Shelf in late March 1912. Reporting on Amundsen's success, the *New York Times* exclaimed, "The whole world has now been discovered." But where was Scott?

Not until the following November did a search party find the three Englishmen side by side in their tent, now a frozen sarcophagus. Nearby was the sledge filled with fossils. The discovery was especially hard on Apsley Cherry-Garrard, who had attempted a search in March, while his friends were still alive, only to turn back at One Ton Camp, unable to properly manage the sled dogs under his command.

Scott's journals and letters electrified the world, making him, not Amundsen, the greater hero, the instant legend. The English press implied that he had died of a broken heart, too dispirited by Amundsen's victory to make the long trek home. "The world largely saw the tale through Scott's eyes," wrote Huntford. "His diaries were rapidly published and, quite simply, he was a better writer than Amundsen. Amundsen lacked the power of advocacy. He was too much the man of action; like so many of his kind, he squandered his talent on his deeds. Living the moment so intensely, he was denied the surplus energy to convey it to others. 'The Last of the Vikings' expected his deeds to speak for themselves."

Amundsen himself was perplexed and saddened by the whole affair. One of his men, Helmer Hanssen, commented, "What shall one say of Scott and his companions who were their own sledge dogs? ...I don't think anyone will ever copy him."

Roland Huntford called Scott a "heroic bungler.... His achievement was to perpetuate the romantic myth of the explorer as martyr and, in a wider sense, to glorify suffering and self-sacrifice as ends in themselves."

But the suffering would continue. While a search party found Scott on the Ross Ice Shelf in November 1912, Douglas Mawson, an Australian geologist, commanded an expedition nearly a thousand miles away in Commonwealth Bay, perhaps the windiest place on earth. With two companions, sledges, and dogs, he traversed the coast of George V Land until one companion disappeared into a crevasse, taking several dogs and important supplies with him. Then the other companion starved to death. It was now mid-January 1913, and Mawson, alone on the ice in the unrelenting wind, would need a miracle to get back alive. Stumbling, crawling, falling into a crevasse and hauling himself out hand over hand, he found a rock

cairn where rescuers had left a food parcel only hours before. When he staggered toward the base hut a week later, his face unrecognizable from frostbite and fatigue, Mawson was greeted by six colleagues who asked, "Which one are you?"

Germany and Japan also sent expeditions south on missions of science and glory. But the man who would emerge as the greatest of Antarctic heroes, whose stature would grow and whose grave site would be visited by pilgrims for decades to come, whose memory would be toasted with Irish whiskey and respect, was neither Mawson nor Amundsen nor Scott, but Ernest Shackleton. He never attained his geographic goals, yet he had a genius for leadership. His new goal, which he announced in 1913, would be "the longest sledge journey ever made," a traverse of Antarctica, more than 2,000 miles from the Weddell Sea to the Ross Sea via the South Pole. He called it the Imperial Trans-Antarctic Expedition. A story made the rounds that he had placed the following notice in the newspaper:

"Men Wanted for Hazardous Journey. Small wages, bitter cold, long months of complete darkness, constant danger, safe return doubtful. Honor and recognition in case of success.—Ernest Shackleton."

But Shackleton had no need to advertise. A simple announcement of his plans in *The Times* on December 29, 1913, brought 5,000 requests to participate. Shackleton's crew would number only 26.

What followed was one of the epic survival stories of the 20th century. Shackleton's ship, the *Endurance,* never reached mainland Antarctica. Trapped in pack ice deep in the Weddell Sea, he and his men drifted northwest for ten months, from January to October 1915, living inside the ship, waiting for spring. When it came, it was cruel, for the shifting pack ice didn't liberate the ship but instead crushed and sank her. For another five months the crew drifted on the sea ice, living in tents, pondering their dark fate, eating whatever seals and penguins they could find, all the while nursing a tiny flame of hope that somehow Shackleton, who never courted despair, would see them through.

In April 1916, with the ice breaking apart beneath and around them, the men took to three small open boats they had off-loaded from the *Endurance* and began to row. Stiff with cold, weak from atrophy and hunger, they battled raging autumn seas in search of safe landfall. "They

VICTORY AT THE SOUTH POLE belonged to Roald Amundsen, who made this photograph of Oscar Wisting (opposite), one of the four men who reached the Pole with him on December 14, 1911. While homeward bound, Amundsen—middle row, third from right—posed with his crew.

made a pitiable sight," wrote Alfred Lansing in his classic book, *Endurance, Shackleton's Incredible Voyage,* "three little boats, packed with the odd remnants of what had once been a proud expedition, bearing twenty-eight suffering men in one final, almost ludicrous bid for survival." Waves lashed them and froze to their clothing and skin. They ran out of fresh water. Days and nights passed like years in a dungeon. They lost an oar. Their fingers and toes froze. Shackleton's voice grew hoarse with fatigue.

Yet they managed to row toward a forsaken fang of black rock called Elephant Island. When the boats finally landed, the men stumbled ashore and fell to the ground. One crewman had a minor heart attack. Others cried with relief. "It was the merest handhold," wrote Lansing, "100 feet wide and 50 feet deep. A meager grip on a savage coast.... But no matter—they were on land. For the first time in 497 days they were on land. Solid, unsinkable, immovable, blessed land."

***ENDURANCE,* ERNEST SHACKLETON'S SHIP,** captured here in the darkness of winter by photographer Frank Hurley, lay icebound for ten months, January to October 1915. The men waited onboard for the Weddell Sea to free their ship. It never did. The *Endurance* was crushed by shifting ice.

FOLLOWING PAGES: In 1988 a crew of four Americans in a 28-foot boat struggled to duplicate Shackleton's crossing of the Drake Passage.

Shackleton now made a difficult decision. Nobody would find them on Elephant Island. Nobody was looking for them. They had long been given up for dead. Somebody would need to go for help. Leaving his second-in-command, Frank Wild, in charge on Elephant Island, Shackleton and five others—Capt. Frank Worsley, second officer Tom Crean, carpenter Harry McNeish, and able seamen Tim McCarthy and John Vincent—shoved off in the 22-foot boat, *James Caird,* to attempt the impossible: an 800-mile crossing of the southern Scotia Sea, the stormiest water in the world, to South Georgia, a speck no more than 25 miles wide. A needle in a haystack.

The expedition had departed from a whaling station there on December 5, 1914. It was now April 24, 1916, Easter Monday. If Shackleton missed South Georgia and blew into the South Atlantic, he would surely die—and take the fate of every crewman with him.

So important was navigation to their survival that Frank Worsley carried the expedition's final chronometer around his neck, keeping it dry at all costs. They made good progress, but fierce winds battered them, and once, in the middle of the night with Shackleton at the tiller, a maverick wave nearly upset them. They lost their sea anchor—critical for holding their bow into the teeth of a gale—and later found their final cask of fresh water tainted and undrinkable. Worsley would kneel in the helmsman's seat, while the others held him steady in rough seas, to shoot the sun with his sextant. Worry and expectation plagued them. Then like a sweet siren, South Georgia was sighted through shifting clouds, and Shackleton said, "We've done it."

According to Lansing, "Feeble, foolish grins spread across their faces, not of triumph or even joy, but simply of unspeakable relief." It truly was a triumph. Among mariners today the journey of the *James Caird* is considered an unmatched feat of navigation and nautical mettle.

Making safe landfall was harrowing, however, and after nearly foundering on offshore rocks, Shackleton and his crew landed on May 10 in King Haakon Bay, on the island's southwest coast, just opposite where they needed to be. Taking the *James Caird* around either end of South Georgia would involve running a gantlet of prevailing winds and rocky shoals. Shackleton considered such a course too risky. So again he decided to do what had never been done before: He and Worsley and Crean would walk over the island to a whaling station.

As they waited for the weather to improve, McNeish, the carpenter,

---

DURING HIS SECOND EXPEDITION to Antarctica in 1934, Richard Byrd camped alone for 4½ months at a weather station on the Ross Ice Shelf. He nearly died from unknowingly inhaling carbon monoxide fumes from a stove and generator.

outfitted their boots with crampon-like nails for glacier travel. They would travel light and fast, with only a small stove, two compasses, binoculars, a carpenter's adz (to use as an ice ax), and a 50-foot climbing rope. No sleeping bags. No tent. No spare gear. Shackleton reasoned that if they didn't make it in 36 hours, they wouldn't make it at all. Nobody had the strength to carry a fully loaded pack anyway; they were exhausted.

Departing at 3:00 a.m., they walked on ice and snow into the clouds. Hours passed, and for a while the going seemed good. But the fog confused them. They descended too early and too far north and had to ascend the glacier again on wobbly legs. They huddled around their stove for a light meal of hoosh and biscuits, then climbed to an estimated 4,500 feet in bitter cold and dying light.

Shackleton straddled a knife-edge ridge and peered into the cloudy unknown where he believed they needed to go—and go fast before they froze to death. He proposed they glissade: join together as a unit and slide like a human sled. Worsley and Crean couldn't believe it. "What if we hit a rock?" Crean asked. "What if the slope doesn't level off?" Worsley asked. "No time for 'what ifs' in the killing cold," Shackleton said.

So they slid, descending a thousand feet in less than three minutes. The temperature warmed; the wind abated. Back on their feet, they contoured across ice and snow, aided by benevolent moonlight. But again the topography and their own eagerness for success duped them into thinking one bay far below was another, and they had to backtrack. Once, while resting, Shackleton jerked his head from sleep, then woke the others, aware they could all easily drift away and freeze to death. Daylight broke as they reached a ridge and heard a distant but unmistakable factory whistle from the whaling station below.

"In that instant," wrote Lansing, "they felt an overwhelming sense of pride and accomplishment. Though they had failed dismally even to come close to the expedition's original objective, they knew now that somehow they had done much, much more than they ever set out to do."

Like a race of men from another world, they walked into Stromness whaling station, unrecognizable with their sooty faces, matted hair, scraggly beards, and tattered clothes. The whalers stared in disbelief. The man in the middle asked the station foreman if he could see the factory manager. The foreman escorted them, as a train of factory workers followed. At the door, the manager, a friend of Shackleton's, stepped back with shock and asked, "Who the hell are you?"

"My name is Shackleton," the man in the middle said.

Some accounts say the manager, an otherwise stolid Norwegian, buried his face in his hands with tears of joy.

It took four attempts with as many boats through icy seas, but Shackleton finally returned to Elephant Island and rescued his men. Not one member of the expedition failed to return home.

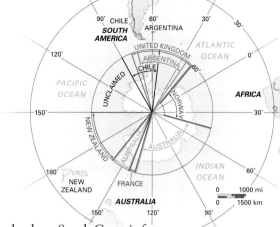

FOLLOWING PAGES: Photographer Galen Rowell shoots a self-portrait in the mirror ball atop the barber pole marking the South Pole, surrounded by flags of Antarctic Treaty nations. The treaty fosters international cooperation, freezing the territorial claims of seven countries (see map at right).

Six years later, in 1922, Shackleton was back on South Georgia for yet another expedition. He suffered a fatal heart attack and was buried there. His widow wanted his final resting place to be in Antarctica. She said the Antarctic had always been his first love.

The South Pole was not visited again until 1929—and then by Richard Byrd and three others in a Ford trimotor monoplane, covering the same distance in 15 hours and 51 minutes that had taken Roald Amundsen three months and had killed Robert Falcon Scott and four companions. Scott had died from lack of food; Byrd jettisoned food to lighten his load.

The mechanized age had arrived in Antarctica. Soon the coast would be defined, the mountains mapped, the Pole inhabited. In 1935 Lincoln Ellsworth made the first successful transantarctic flight, running out of fuel only 16 miles shy of Byrd's old base, Little America.

In 1939 a secret mission by the Third Reich conducted aerial surveys of Antarctica and dropped aluminum darts engraved with swastikas to lay claim to territory. And in 1947 Operation Highjump, organized by the U.S. Navy, brought 4,700 men, 13 ships, and 23 aircraft to Antarctica.

During the International Geophysical Year of 1957-58, concerned scientists from 67 countries joined efforts to secure a future of peaceful cooperation in Antarctica. Scientific stations proliferated then, among them the U.S. Amundsen-Scott Station at the South Pole. But most significant was the birth of the Antarctic Treaty, an unprecedented document in human affairs that held in abeyance all territorial claims.

Amid all this, Ernest Shackleton's dream of a successful crossing of the continent did come true in 1958 when Vivian Fuchs (aided by Edmund Hillary, of Mount Everest fame) commanded the Commonwealth Trans-Antarctic Expedition and became the first to reach the South Pole overland since Scott and his men 46 years earlier. Using modified farm tractors and air reconnaissance, the expedition covered 2,158 miles from the Weddell Sea to the Ross Sea in 99 days. Hillary nearly ran out of fuel, and Fuchs struggled through labyrinthine crevasses. But in the end they prevailed.

Reflecting on those who had come before him to the white continent, Hillary said: "For scientific leadership give me Scott; for swift and efficient travel, Amundsen; but…in a hopeless situation, when there seems no way out, get down on your knees and pray for Shackleton." ∎

CHAPTER THREE

Late for Dinner
Penguins, Petrels, Seals, and Whales

April brings darkness to Antarctica. The sun winks away. A brittle moon rises, bright but without warmth on a growing apron of floating sea ice that surrounds the continent, doubling its size. The freezer door slams shut. It's time to get out, go north, find sustenance if not safety in the adjacent storm-tossed southern ocean. Adélie, chinstrap, and gentoo penguins—all closely related—have finished breeding. Another generation has survived the odds. Another fleeting austral summer has come and gone, taking all hospitality with it. Rookeries once filled with raucous, boisterous life are now silent. They belong to the wind and snow. Newly fledged penguins, out to sea for the first time, will find it arduous. Many will meet predators or starvation. Yet few of them—none in fact— would survive a winter on the continent.

But every rule has its exception, and among the penguins of Antarctica that exception stands nearly 4 feet tall, weighs 70 to

AN EMPEROR PENGUIN CHICK receives a nuzzle from its devoted parent. If all goes well, the chick will molt into juvenile plumage at five months, become sexually mature at four years, and join the roughly 195,000 emperor penguin pairs that breed in Antarctica.

80 pounds, wears a regal suit of white, blue-gray, black, and yellow, and arrives on the fast ice (sea ice attached to land) after everyone else has gone. It is the emperor penguin, largest of the 17 species of penguins. It is, writes biologist David G. Campbell, "a wholly oceanic species—indeed, the only species of bird that need never alight on land in the course of its life."

Having feasted heavily in March and April (the austral autumn), the emperors burst from the sea onto the ice shelf and begin a long trek of up to 75 miles, alternately walking and tobogganing on their bellies at half a mile an hour, following instincts seemingly as old as Antarctica itself. Having fattened on fish, squid, and krill over summer, the emperors at this time can weigh 20 pounds more than average (upwards of 100 pounds).

They will need it for their courting at the start of winter. A single egg is laid in late May and early June amid howling winds, utter darkness, and unspeakable cold. No nest. The emperor female lays the egg and quickly transfers it to her mate, who cradles it on his feet and covers it with a downy undercoat of abdominal skin beneath thick feathers—80 per square inch—layered like roof shingles for optimum insulation. While the female returns to sea to feed, for the next 62 to 66 days—the entire incubation period—the male resolutely protects the egg, cradling it on his feet as he huddles on the ice with thousands of others for warmth and protection. "They're like people in a crisis," says seabird ecologist Graham Robertson. "They forget their differences and rally together." Some emperor colonies number a few hundred birds; some number more than 60,000.

The chicks hatch in July and early August, after each fasting male has lost one-third to one-half of his body weight. Yet even then he finds the strength to give his chick a regurgitated secretion of fat and protein held in his crop for more than two months. At this critical time, with the male exhausted from starvation and exposure to cold, the female arrives. She's been feeding at sea for two months and has the fat to prove it. The chick snuggles into her brood pouch and eats its first fresh food. A routine develops, with male and female alternately feeding at sea and cradling the chick, commuting to and fro every few days with unflagging devotion. The sun rises but brings no warmth. Winds howl. All the while, the chick rests cocooned in the brood pouch of one of its parents. If it tumbled out, it would freeze to death in two minutes.

Spring advances, the ice sheet retreats and the parents' commute shortens in perfect proportion to the growing appetite of the chick. The ingenuity of this breeding system now becomes clear, for as the ice apron shrinks and breaks into floes, the young birds are carried out to sea just as they molt into their diving plumage. Should spring be late and the sea ice persist, the young emperors will die of starvation. Should the ice melt too fast, the chicks will fall into the sea before growing proper feathers.

Survival is a thin edge here, with little margin for miscalculation. The only guarantee is risk itself. Little wonder, then, that penguins who survive into adulthood seem exultant about it. They lift their dagger beaks and trumpet to the sky. They've beaten the odds. They gather on phantasmagoric icebergs and punctuate the ice with the power of an exclamation point. Here we are! Here we have been for many thousands of years—and shall remain. Against the cold austerity of ice and rock, their voices seem every bit as profound as a Socratic injunction.

Rare is the visitor who can stand before penguins unmoved, who is not awestruck by their numbers and elegance and ability to survive—to thrive, in fact—in such a cold place. Antarctic conservationist Ron Naveen says the endearing character of penguins will turn even the most dispassionate observer into a "raving anthropomorphic."

In his book, *The Worst Journey in the World,* explorer Apsley Cherry-Garrard wrote of penguins: "They are extraordinarily like children, these little people of the Antarctic world, either like children, or like old men, full of their own importance and late for dinner, in their black tail-coats and white shirt-fronts—and rather portly withal." Ecologist Bernard Stonehouse says, "I have often had the impression that, to penguins, man is just another penguin—different, less predictable, occasionally violent, but tolerable company when he sits still and minds his own business."

So confused were early explorers by the sight of penguins—strange creatures that swam with great agility, that porpoised through the sea but couldn't fly—they classified them as fish. Yet penguins laid eggs and, upon careful inspection, were found to have feathers, albeit small ones. Finally regarded as birds, penguins were then relegated to the status of primitive. The purpose of the 1911 winter journey from Cape Evans to Cape Crozier by Edward Wilson, Henry Bowers, and Apsley Cherry-Garrard, three men in Capt. Robert Falcon Scott's expedition, was to gather emperor eggs to prove (or disprove) by examining the embryos that penguins were primitive phylogenetic links between birds and reptiles.

We now understand penguins for what they truly are: not clumsy misfits but animals exquisitely adapted to their world, birds not at the bottom of a branch in the evolutionary tree of life but at the top. Author, naturalist, and film producer Tony Soper says penguins are "superbly designed for their job, flying underwater with great skill. Their compact, streamlined bodies have a deep keel for a breastbone and massive paddle

FOLLOWING PAGES: An emperor penguin bursts from the sea onto the ice. For a brief moment its flippers seem wings again, as it mimics flying.

ARTFUL SWIMMERS, emperor penguins hunt for fish and squid and typically dive as deep as 160 feet, though dives below 800 feet are not uncommon. The longest recorded dive for an emperor is 18 minutes. Negotiating slippery slopes (opposite) can be difficult for emperors. Often these penguins find it easier tobogganing on their bellies than staying upright on their feet.

muscles. Their feathers are reduced in size and stiffened with fluffy after-shafts. This down creates an insulating layer of air over a thick layer of blubber and skin. Their heads retract to create a perfect hydrodynamic shape.... Their wings are reduced to paddles, and bones flattened, with the wrist and elbow joints fused, so that although the wing can't be folded, it acts as a powerful propulsion unit. The legs are set well back on the body so that the feet act as control surfaces in the water. Some walk, some progress by jumps, some by tobogganing over ice and snow. Some can climb steep cliff faces, some leap like salmon in order to land on ice floes." And all have white fronts and black backs, coloration that helps prevent detection by predators (primarily leopard seals and killer whales). From above they blend into the darkness of the deep sea. From below they blend into the brightness of the sky.

All seventeen species of penguins are restricted to the Southern Hemisphere, the northernmost living in the Galápagos Islands, on the Equator, sustained there by upwelling and the presence of the cold Humboldt Current. Only seven species breed south of the Antarctic Convergence: two tall penguins—emperor and king of the genus *Aptenodytes*; three "brush-tails"—Adélie, chinstrap, and gentoo of the genus *Pygoscelis*; and two crested—macaroni and rockhopper of the genus *Eudyptes* (rockhoppers only just inside the Convergence, at Heard Island).

Like emperors, king penguins walk slowly, swim swiftly, wear ornate gold about the head and neck, and the female lays one egg. While emperors breed on ice deep in the freezer, kings prefer subantarctic islands, still in the refrigerator, but farther north where conditions are less austere. Gathering in colonies in great numbers (some upwards of 200,000), they make an unforgettable scene, calling, whistling, head-flagging, slapping each other with their flipperlike wings. On South Georgia, which has been called "a lonely outcrop in the middle of a protein extravaganza," they stand on raised beach shelves backdropped by serrated mountains and alpine glaciers, drinking from meltwater rivers that run through the colony. Because chicks require more than a year to fledge, kings breed only once every two years (although efficient parents may raise two young every three years). Chicks appear anything but regal. Dressed in their shaggy brown coat, they were once considered a separate species, the woolly penguin.

EMPEROR PENGUINS, all in a row, cradle on their feet one big gray chick each. Like king penguins, emperors lay only one egg and hold it atop their feet; chinstraps lay two eggs in a pebble nest. A chinstrap penguin chick (opposite) begins to emerge after 35 to 38 days in the egg, watched carefully by its parent.

To judge penguins only on land would be unfair. At sea, all awkwardness is abandoned as kings routinely dive to 150 feet, and at times more than 750 feet, in pursuit of fish and squid. Smaller penguin species dart after krill with an agility as impressive as that of swallows in the sky. They can swim at a sustained rate of up to 15 miles an hour, with short sprints even faster. Adélies, chinstraps, and gentoos burst from the sea to land on the ice; macaronis and rockhoppers do the same, more likely to land on steep rocky cliffs, sometimes leaping from storm waves that break fiercely on headlands. Slammed against the rocks, the tough macaronis shake their heads and begin the long climb to their nests. Sharp claws on their toes afford them good traction. Rockhoppers do as their name implies; they hop, often up precipitous slopes with fearless determination. Like macaronis, they largely inhabit subantarctic islands and have brilliant straw-yellow feathered crests above their eyes. "Macaroni" comes from 18th-century England; explorers of a later period said the penguins reminded them of foppish young Englishmen who traveled to Italy, dyed

UNABLE TO FEED AT SEA for themselves, ever hungry penguin chicks must rely on regurgitated food from their parents. Young chinstraps (above) pursue a provider for the "stuff" to sustain life. Two emperor chicks (below) appear to discuss affairs of the stomach while waiting for a meal. An older king penguin chick, dressed in brown down (opposite), begs for a meal from its parent.

their hair in colorful streaks, and belonged to the Macaroni Club.

An estimated five million pairs of macaroni penguins breed on South Georgia. Others, in smaller numbers, breed as far south as the northern tip of the Antarctic Peninsula. They court by shaking their golden plumes wildly. They bray hoarsely into the salt wind and collect small pebbles for their nests. Like rockhoppers, a breeding pair of macaronis lays two eggs, the first one smaller than the second, and incubates them for 34 to 35 days. The smaller egg usually fails; if the chick hatches, it soon dies. Should the summer be bountiful, the smaller chick will prosper into adulthood, though it seldom happens.

Many years are lean. Among the brushtails, which lay two eggs, only one nest in ten typically sees two chicks raised to fledglings. Then comes the first winter at sea and additional mortality. The Adélie is a true Antarctic penguin, living mainly on the continent or on nearby islands. The gentoo is a more subantarctic species, found as far north as the Falkland Islands. Occupying the middle ground is the feisty and successful chinstrap, at home both on the continent and on several islands.

Male Adélies will walk 60 miles over fast ice in the spring to reach their breeding areas. Females follow in search of a familiar nest site and a mate. Tony Soper observes that in Adélies the pair-bond is less strong than in other brushtails (gentoos and chinstraps): "The harsh requirements of the short season allow for no delay. The imperative is to begin courtship, and the male will bond quickly with an available female rather than delay in waiting for last year's mate. Courtship is brief, with much flipper waving and guttural gossip." Incubation can be as short as 30 days or as long as 43, depending on local conditions.

Unlike emperors and kings, brushtails gather pebbles to build elevated nests above surrounding meltwater. The pebble market involves a daily drama of neighborhood theft, bickering, and home improvement, as pebbles move from nest to nest amid jealous, redemptive parents who artfully steal from others but decry the injustice when it happens to them.

Adélie chicks hatch in late December, fledge in 50 to 56 days, and go to sea by mid-February, just as swarms of krill occur near shore. Chinstraps and gentoos hatch and fledge later, as their season is not so cold or truncated. While gentoos on the Antarctic Peninsula fledge in 62 to 82 days and are smaller, those in northern, gentler climes (on subantarctic islands) take 85 to 117 days. Northern gentoos can in fact replace a lost clutch—rare among penguins. As late as March, a full month after young Adélies have gone to sea to take care of themselves, newly fledged northern gentoos will tarry on shore and accept food from their parents.

In many penguin colonies the dark, fierce birds called skuas (sometimes mistaken for juvenile gulls) lord it over the penguins with despotic aeronautics, strafing the tuxedoed crowd, wheeling suddenly to drop onto

FOLLOWING PAGES: Members of the most abundant and widespread of all albatross species, two black-browed albatrosses greet on South Georgia. Populations may total 600,000.

a lone or abandoned chick. Larger than most gulls, skuas have sharp beaks, similar to those of hawks. The brown skua, one of two species in Antarctica, thinks little of diving at humans and on rare occasion has knocked a person unconscious. The skua is also a pirate. Known to pursue terns and shags and grab their tails or wings in flight, it forces them to disgorge a meal, then snatches the falling morsel before it hits the water.

At scientific stations, skuas forage through garbage bins and befriend researchers who make a habit of feeding them. "Skuas are the berserkers among birds," wrote ornithologist Robert Cushman Murphy. "They seem to have a diabolical gift to be a scourge…. But in spite of their voracity, rapine and cannibalism, the skuas quickly make themselves the beneficiaries of…anthropomorphic interest. When they crowd around you, and look up with bright, fearless, unsuspicious brown eyes, accept the bounty you offer them, and show no more concern over the loudest shouts, whistles, or handclaps than if they were stone deaf, you succumb to their charm, and subscribe to the principle that their supremacy of might must be deserved." The other species, the south polar skua, is the most southerly bird in the world, and has been seen at the South Pole. It feeds primarily on krill and some fish, yet it also depends on piracy and penguin predation and even takes adult Wilson's storm-petrels in flight.

As penguin chicks grow and have greater nutritional needs, both parents must leave the nest and go to sea to feed them. The chicks then gather in nursery groups, called crèches, and find safety and warmth in numbers. Skuas that before could easily attack isolated small chicks that wandered off a nest, now face a greater challenge: The chicks are larger, full of fight, and stand en masse as a sea of bobbing heads. A sudden snowstorm followed by chilling winds can kill young penguins, and the skuas remain alert for that possibility. So the penguins huddle, those on the periphery always jostling for better positions inside, making the crèche a dynamic crowd of rising and falling fortunes.

Skuas are not alone in patroling penguin rookeries on the Antarctic Peninsula. Enter the snowy sheathbill, a contradictory bird that dresses in white, yet collects garbage; is reluctant to fly, yet in fact has strong flight; has unwebbed feet and looks like a pigeon, yet makes its living second-hand from the sea. The sheathbill eats penguin feces, seal placentas,

broken eggs, spilled krill—almost anything organic—and may use team-work to get it. While one sheathbill distracts an adult penguin feeding its chick, causing the regurgitated krill to land on the ground, another sheath-bill quickly steals it. The penguin brays in protest, but to no avail.

Other kinds of emotional vocalization by penguins were witnessed by naturalist Tui de Roy on volcanic Deception Island, near the Antarctic Peninsula. She observed chinstraps in "…moments of dramatic personal significance in their private lives. There were instances of emotional reunions or intense struggle, quiet family scenes and cases of sheer per-plexity." Describing two of the birds starting a fight, she says: "Outrage spread through the squawking neighborhood. Together the quarreling birds tumbled down a scree embankment before the matter was finally settled. They stood up at last, shook themselves and walked off. One moved down the valley, looking nervous and unsettled, while the other, indignant, returned to its nest." There is no court of law in a penguin breed-ing colony, no cop on a beat, no random act of kindness. The short and stressful breeding season underscores every Malthusian law of survival.

As if to compensate for penguins' not being able to fly airborne, the Antarctic boasts an impressive array of champion flyers among the world's seabirds—albatrosses and their smaller cousins, petrels, legendary birds that wing over waves in gale-force winds, artfully soaring amid salt spray and whitecaps. Many species follow ships for days on end; and one, the wandering albatross, with a wingspan of 10 to 11 feet, may circle the globe in its search for food. These great feathered mariners are to the southern seas what grizzly bears, wolves, and caribou are to northern lands: ultimate travelers, totemic to a degree, always a thrill to see.

"Nearby," wrote Robert Cushman Murphy, who sailed the southern oceans in the early 1900s, "flew the long-awaited fowl, even more majes-tic, more supreme, than my imagination had pictured…. They would fly again and again across the quarterdeck, jerking up their heads like spir-ited steeds and showing curiosity and temptation in every action…. Dur-ing brisk breezes they zoomed across the stern close enough for me to see the color of their eyes and hear the humming of their stiff quills…. I now belong to a higher cult of mortals, for I have seen the albatross."

Six species of albatrosses and eighteen species of petrels breed near or below the Antarctic Convergence, nearly all on subantarctic islands. Creatures of sea and sky, they seem a union of the two, utterly at home in wind and water, an environment that tosses ships like flotsam. They spend much of their lives in flight, gliding and soaring—so much so that Mur-phy said they were the birds that made the wind blow. If they didn't have to breed, they wouldn't come to shore. But they do, and so for a few moments they are in our element. To approach a wandering albatross on its nest is to feel a deep sense of regard. It mates for life, can live 50 years, does not begin to breed until age 10, and lays only one egg every two years,

WORLD'S GREATEST GLIDER, the wandering albatross rides the wind on a wingspan of more than ten feet. Of the world population of wanderers, estimated at 37,000 pairs, more than 4,000 pairs breed on South Georgia.

incubating it for 78 days. When a wandering albatross returns to its nest to greet its mate after ten days at sea, the pair clack their long, hooked bills in exquisite gentleness. They bow, dance, strut, and gape with such poetry and élan that they beg a suspension of the human prejudice that our species alone experiences passion and love.

South Georgia is a mecca for albatrosses. Four species breed there: the wandering, the black-browed, the grey-headed, and the light-mantled sooty. Dressed in elegant French gray with a pale blue lateral groove on the lower mandible and a white semicircle around the eye, the light-mantled sooty sky-points amid tussock grass and calls *p'yarrr-eee* as its mate flies overhead. Other sooties might fly by, but they receive no evocative call, for each bird reserves it for its mate.

Black-browed and grey-headed albatrosses are mollymawks, a collective term for medium-size albatrosses with wingspans of seven to eight feet. "Mollymawk" comes from the Dutch *mal,* meaning "foolish," and *mok,*

THIS BROWN SKUA BERATING a female wandering albatross will later back off from the mismatched fight. A grey-headed albatross protects its chick (opposite), which requires about 141 days of care from hatching to fledging.

meaning "gull." As Tony Soper has observed, "These pejorative and richly undeserved epithets were the result partly of seeing albatrosses ashore, out of their element, appearing clumsy, and partly because of their endearing but ill-advised innocence in standing quietly while being bludgeoned by a club and picked up for the pot."

Out to sea on an indigo night, soaring over inky water, an albatross sees bioluminescing squid below. It alights and feeds by surface-seizing and shallow plunging, raking its long bill into its prey. It then spreads its wings and is airborne again, surfing the wind. Anything but clumsy.

Because early seafarers believed the souls of fellow sailors were reincarnated as albatrosses, it was considered bad luck to kill one. An albatross that lived beyond its first year—a time of high mortality—could until recently count on a long life. But now a rapidly expanding commercial squid fishery in the southern seas kills albatrosses by the thousands: some in gillnets, others hooked on longlines. A few choke on plastic rubbish. Still others become conditioned to eating food thrown from boats, then may starve to death when the boats don't return. Worldwide, albatross numbers are declining by one percent per year—a recipe for disaster.

No less wondrous than the great wandering albatross is its smallest southern cousin, the Wilson's storm-petrel. An elegant dark bird with a conspicuous white rump and square tail, this little dancer (hardly bigger

REGURGITATION—FOR THE BIRDS. Wandering albatrosses feed chicks by regurgitating stomach oil and partly digested squid and fish. Incubation and fledging take more than a year, so the birds lay one egg every two years. The low reproductive rate makes them slow to respond to environmental change.

than a large sparrow, with a 7-inch body and 16-inch wingspan) flies like a butterfly as it skips and patters over the surface of the sea, wings upright, legs dangling. It can appear to fly backward for brief moments, prompting Peruvians to call it *bailarína,* or "dancer." Although most people will never see one, it is perhaps the most numerous seabird in the world, with a total population well into the millions. It tries to come ashore to breed under cover of darkness, wary of gulls and skuas that prey upon it. After breeding, the female smells its way to an island burrow or crevice where she lays a single extraordinarily large egg.

The more commonly seen pintado petrel (also called cape pigeon) is also black and white, with a sooty head, but wears its colors with an artist's abandon: white spattered on a black back. Pintados often follow ships throughout the southern seas, where they are abundant. Flying in small flocks, they make a memorable sight. Storms can kill many younger birds, and skuas take a few. Yet, if a pintado survives into breeding age, it can live 15 to 20 years.

Among southbound birders who keep a life list, two of the greatest prizes are the antarctic petrel and the snow petrel—birds of the ice, most likely seen in the Ross Sea. While the antarctic petrel might be mistaken from afar for a pintado (but is slightly larger and slimmer, with elegant lines of black and white on the wings) the snow petrel is all white with obsidian eyes and bill. Every spring, snow petrels fly high into the mountains and nunataks of coastal Antarctica, where in loose colonies they breed in rocky hollows and crevices. Surrounded by a crystal sea of glacial ice, they seem to us frightfully alone in a prebiotic world.

When a snow petrel collided with a ship and was injured beyond repair, a crew member handed it to David G. Campbell, who wrote, "Holding it is like touching animate warm ice.... A denizen of the cold, it can't survive indoor temperatures. How alien to my physiology is this little creature, forever bound to the frozen pole, as I am forever imperiled by it.... Grounded, it won't survive long…, nor does it have a future living with humans. Today a brown skua, also born this season, alights a few meters away and patiently watches the petrel flail. It has the calm patience of a scavenger. After the skua leaves, I drop the petrel into the sea. It floats on the calm water that it can never leave, tucks its feathers, and paddles away."

A great contradiction of Antarctica is that while the continent itself is largely sterile—98 percent covered in ice, the rest supporting only two species of flowering plants, a grass and a pink, and many mosses and lichens—the surrounding ocean is the most fertile on earth. Similar to the tropics where intense year-round sunlight creates upper water layers of lighter density that cannot mix with deeper, colder, nutrient-rich layers, the Antarctic summer brings strong thermal stratification to the southern oceans. Melting ice creates a warmer, less saline sea surface (especially in the productive east-wind drift, a circumpolar current).

Due to local turbulence and upwelling, waters mix more readily, and nutrients flush to the surface. Long days of spring arrive, bringing light, the elixir of life, and Antarctic waters erupt with trillions of single-celled algae called phytoplankton. The algae occur not just in the sea but also in the pack ice. The most important of these are diatoms, characterized by each cell's being encased in a little hydrated silicon shell, shaped like a pillbox. Feeding on the algae are zooplankton—amphipods, copepods, ctenophores, mystids, and shrimplike krill—which in turn are eaten by fish, squid, birds, seals, and whales.

One species in particular, antarctic krill *(Euphausia superba),* exists in greater biomass than any other species on earth, estimated at more than a

billion tons. In one of the shortest and most efficient food chains in the world, an adult blue whale consumes three to four tons of krill every day in the course of a four-month austral summer. Entire breeding colonies of Adélie penguins subsist on krill. The most abundant seal in the world, the misnamed crabeater, eats almost nothing but krill, each crabeater consuming 20 to 25 times its body weight a year.

If krill were distributed evenly through the ocean, they would fail to sustain such numbers. But they cluster along ice margins where algae grow. They swarm. Like great blizzards in the sea, krill mass together and provide bountiful buffets for penguins, seals, and whales. Some swarms measure more than 10 miles long, 5 miles wide, and 100 yards deep. A cubic yard of this seawater can contain more than 10,000 krill. Whaling skippers once hunted their prey by studying the color of the sea, watching for the green hues of algae and the prized pink of krill, which meant that whales would not be far away. Were it not for krill, Antarctica would have vastly fewer numbers of the half million whales, the 100 million penguins, and the 20 million seals it now has.

And the future? Krill may be artificially abundant in Antarctica in the wake of 60 years of intense 20th-century whaling. Some scientists believe crabeater seals and brushtailed penguins—both more common than in prewhaling days—now eat as many krill as do all remaining southern baleen whales. In the decades following the demise of commercial whaling, some populations of Adélie penguins increased 3 to 4 percent per year, and some chinstrap populations 7 to 10 percent. Nobody knows precisely what the prehuman Antarctic ecosystem contained: more whales, certainly, and probably fewer seals and penguins.

The entire system revolves around krill. Rich in protein, they can live seven years and reproduce at high rates. An adult female spawns 16 times a season, each time producing up to 2,000 eggs. But reproduction comes at a cost. The bioluminescent sexual organs that krill use to attract one another also attract predators, including Russian, Eastern European, and Japanese commercial trawlers who shine bright night-lights into the sea, then drop large nets and harvest close to half a million tons of krill a year. This exploitation would be higher were it not for fluorine in krill shells, an element beneficial to humans in small amounts (for fighting cavities in

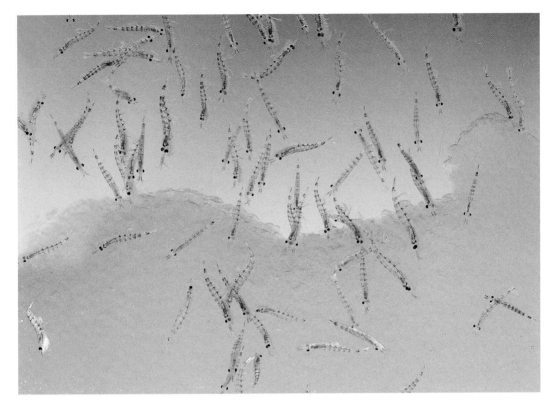

STAFF OF LIFE, krill sustain whales, seals, and penguins. Adult antarctic krill measure about 2.5 inches. Beneath a krill's black eye (opposite) a "filter basket" enclosed in its front legs captures algae from seawater.

teeth) but toxic in large amounts. When krill die and decompose, fluorine migrates rapidly from the indigestible chitin shell into the soft digestible meat, and becomes potentially lethal for all who ingest it. The elevated body temperature of penguins and seals denatures the fluorine, releasing enzymes that enable these creatures to store it in their bones and eventually excrete it. Not so humans. Experiments are under way to produce a low-fluorine krill paste that is marketable as a "protein panacea." If successful, krill could become a major new target species. Humans have never previously cast their nets into a fishery so low on the marine food chain. It's one thing to harvest from the top, removing predators such as salmon, whales, and seals. It's another to remove huge volumes of krill, upon which nearly everything else depends.

The crabeater seal, for example, eats krill, which early explorers mistook for crabs. Once considered rare because it inhabits Antarctic pack ice and is seldom seen, the crabeater is now considered the most abundant marine mammal on earth, numbering more than 15 million. There

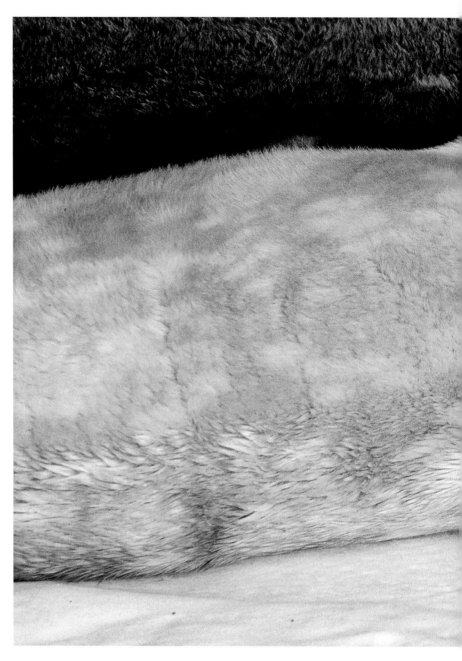

PRECEDING PAGES: A leopard seal, master predator of fish, penguins, and crabeater seals, displays its lethal teeth to an Adélie penguin who keeps its distance. Those same teeth can puncture inflatable boats—and have—giving scientists and tourists a thrill they don't care to repeat.

WEDDELL SEAL PUP finds comfort against its mother's body on the Antarctic ice. Throughout the austral winter (April-October) Weddell seals remain on or below the ice, in search of food and breathing holes (opposite). Pups weigh 60 pounds at birth but grow quickly on mother's milk, which contains more than 40 percent fat. Within seven weeks of their birth, pups can dive to 300 feet.

are probably more crabeaters than all other seals combined. In summer, crabeaters appear alone or in pairs on loose pack ice, or sometimes they swim in packs—an impressive sight—to increase hunting efficiency. Their long rows of multilobed teeth are perfectly adapted for straining krill. As post-whaling numbers of krill multiplied, crabeaters—able to capture a larger share of the bounty—reduced their age of maturity, which resulted, many scientists think, in larger populations of crabeaters in Antarctica. Given their recent success and that of krill-eating penguins, it is uncertain whether baleen whales, once the great consumers of krill, will return to Antarctic waters in the vast numbers they maintained a century ago.

Leopard seals also eat krill, but are more noteworthy for cruising off-shore penguin colonies, grabbing the birds and thrashing them violently back and forth, flailing them out of their skins and devouring them. The penguin skins and attached limb bones wash ashore and fit human hands like mittens, skin on the outside, feathers on the inside, bones picked clean of meat. With its sinister mouth, snakelike head, and violence toward penguins, the leopard seal is the "bad boy" of the Antarctic. Passengers on ships report seeing them asleep on loose pack ice, usually solitary, waking up as the ship passes, their mouths open in anger as if not even a five-story-tall, 250-foot-long steel vessel is off the menu. They seldom attack humans. Yet, there *are* stories.

A leopard seal harassed two scuba divers in Arthur Harbor, near America's Palmer Station, for 45 minutes in 1974. A Zodiac driver finally rescued them. Another instance had occurred in 1915 when a huge leopard seal threatened a member of the Shackleton expedition who was hunting on the Weddell Sea pack ice. When he fled, the seal pursued him from beneath the shallow ice. When Frank Wild, the expedition's second-in-command, came to the rescue with a rifle, the seal emerged to turn on him. Luckily, Wild was able to fire before the seal reached him.

Roughly one-third of a leopard seal's diet is penguins and krill. The rest is other seals, primarily crabeater pups, which suffer high mortality in the spring. Up to 80 percent of adult crabeaters have scars down their flanks from narrowly escaping in early life the leopard seal's massive canine teeth.

Four of the six species of seals found in Antarctica give birth on ice: the crabeater, leopard, Weddell, and Ross. The other two, the antarctic fur seal and the southern elephant seal, breed on beaches, and with great drama, as they practice a hierarchical mating system where large bulls command a shore and gather all females who arrive there to give birth and breed again. Their new pups born, the females are quickly claimed and impregnated by the dominant bull—a beach master—who has vanquished all other males. The beach master elephant seal can defend upward of 100 females; a fur seal, 30 to 40 females. The other males, licking their wounds, are doomed to bachelorhood and must suffer the insult of not having offspring. Size, strength and moxie are thus critical to the success of every

FOLLOWING PAGES: Four king penguins "confer" amid a jousting match between two southern elephant seals, the world's largest seal species, on a beach on South Georgia.

male fur seal and elephant seal. A female elephant seal that weighs one ton—not exactly a featherweight—is dwarfed by her beach master that weighs four times more: 8,000 pounds.

The other four seal species exhibit little or no sexual dimorphism (outward physical differences between male and female). Females of these species are in fact slightly larger than the males, since they must produce milk for their young. They have no rigid territories, harems, or beach masters that trample pups in blind pursuit of challengers. Conditions on the pack ice are more severe. Parental care is abbreviated.

Opposite in disposition to the leopard seal, the Weddell seal wears what looks like a faint smile on its small face. It is the most southerly mammal in the world, found almost exclusively in the fast ice, as far south as 78° S. All antarctic seals are accomplished divers, but the Weddell excels. A typical dive lasts 15 minutes, as the seal descends 900 to 1,300 feet to prey on antarctic cod weighing up to 70 pounds. This cod is a benthic fish that makes up nearly 60 percent of the Weddell seal's diet. A longer dive can last more than an hour. When the seal surfaces under winter ice, it uses forward-pointing upper incisors and canines and swings its head back and forth to enlarge a breathing hole.

Southern elephant seals dive even deeper, going down as far as 3,000 feet into the lightless basement of Antarctica. They stay down for about 30 minutes and eat mostly squid, which they can see because squid bioluminesce. To fathom a seal's ability to dive so deep and long, consider its physiology. It stores oxygen not only in the hemoglobin of its red blood cells but also in the myoglobin of muscle tissue. And while human bodies are by weight 7 percent blood, seals are 12 percent blood, further increasing their store of oxygen. (That adds up to 900 pounds of blood for a large bull.) Before diving, a seal exhales, purging itself of atmospheric nitrogen, which causes crippling bends during rapid ascent after a deep dive. At a depth of 3,000 feet, the pressure is 90 times greater than at sea level. The lungs collapse. The heart slows to nearly a stop. The skull flexes but does not break. Amid it all, the seal hunts and feeds, gorging itself to build up blubber reserves that enable it to fast for up to eight weeks while on land.

The deep black sea is the elephant seal's grandest stage—the environment where so many marvelous adaptations come into play, hidden

SOUTHERN ELEPHANT SEALS lounge together on a beach on Livingston Island, in the South Shetlands. The seals come ashore to mate and, in late summer, to molt (opposite, above). Old hair is shed for new, a process that takes about 40 days. The seals then return to the sea, their true element, where they dive a thousand feet and more in search of squid and fish.

FOLLOWING PAGES: Nearly hunted to extinction in the early 1800s, antarctic fur seals have rebounded—with exuberance—along the north coast of South Georgia.

ANTARCTIC FUR SEAL gives birth. While most pups are born dark, a few are white (opposite). Fur seals belong to the family *Otariidae,* which, unlike the true seals, have external ears and can rotate their hind limbs for locomotion on land.

from our eyes if not our imaginations. Back on the beach, life is more a backstage affair for these animals, full of socializing and pinniped debauchery. They lounge with their kin, packed tightly together side by side, belching and bellowing, scratching their flanks with their flippers, flipping sand onto their backs. They come ashore twice each year: first in early spring (September/October) to give birth and mate; then again in late summer (January/February) to molt—shed old hair for new. It is during the molt that they are most gregarious.

Mating season finds every large elephant seal bull on the beach, head held high, trumpeting his dominance through his inflated, bulbous nose, or proboscis, convinced he's the toughest of the tough. His scarred neck testifies to the many battles he's endured with other like-minded bulls. So strenuous are these battles that many bulls limp away, severely injured, and die of their wounds. Meanwhile, the female, who has lost more than 300 pounds during four weeks of lactation (while her pup has gained 10 to 15 pounds a day), is half starved but nonetheless able to mate before her pup is fully weaned. Unaided by either parent, the weaned pup must then find its own way to the sea and learn to swim and hunt.

Elephant seals and fur seals were ruthlessly hunted by man: elephant seals for their thick blubber to be rendered into oil, fur seals for their fur. Not until the mid-1960s did sealing—and shore-based whaling—end in the Antarctic. Although seals have recovered by the hundreds of thousands, their populations are genetically impoverished. Each seal today is descended from only a few survivors that somehow escaped club and knife. Although possessed of his or her own individuality, each fur seal today is more closely related to its kin than its ancestors were before the slaughter. In a world of ozone holes, greenhouse gases, and other growing environmental stresses, wildlife populations possess few tools more valuable for survival and for fighting disease than deep, diverse gene pools. These seals simply don't have the gene pool they once did.

Neither do the great whales.

"Beyond 40 degrees is no law," whalers once said in the southern seas, "beyond 50 degrees, no God." Had they plundered scarcity as well as they did abundance, there would be no whales at all. The leviathans survived, but whale populations have not significantly rebounded. Whales reproduce slowly, and the krill and small fish on which many whales feast have been claimed by expanded numbers of penguins and crabeater seals.

Eleven species of whales occupy Antarctic waters, six of them baleen whales: the blue, the sei, the fin, the humpback, the minke, and the southern right. The others are toothed whales: the sperm, the Arnoux's beaked, and the southern bottlenose. The killer whale and the hourglass dolphin, also toothed, are members of the dolphin family. Cetologist Kenneth S. Norris describes baleen whales as "huge, toothless mammals that feed by filtering seawater of vast quantities of planktonic sea life, schools of small crustaceans, and schooling fish. Scientists term these whales the mysticetes (Latin for 'mustached whale,' a reference to the straining mechanism of sieve plates, or baleen, that hang from the roof of a baleen whale's mouth and by means of which it captures food). Baleen plates resemble porous, fibrous curtains. The whale's huge tongue presses the mouthfuls of water through the baleen to sieve out its prey." The right whale and the sei actually swim through swarms of krill and copepods, mouths wide open, skimming their prey. Their own forward motion, not their tongues, pushes the seawater through their baleen.

Whale baleen is composed of keratin, the same substance as in human fingernails and hair. It differs in coarseness and size from species to species, according to diet. Because the southern right whale eats mostly tiny copepods, it has dense baleen with plates so long that they must fold in half for the mouth to close. Fin and blue whales, which prefer adolescent and adult krill and adolescent krill respectively, have baleen made of finer bristles for larger prey. All southern baleen whales attain great body length— nearly 100 feet for the blue, 90 feet for the fin, 60 feet for the right, 50 feet for the humpback—and were assumed by early whalers and explorers to have long lives as well, like sequoias and redwoods. They do not. They live 25 to 40 years, growing fast but reproducing slowly. (The age of mysticete whales is determined by counting the growth layers in an extension of the eardrum; toothed whales, by dentin growth rings.) Come winter, the whales migrate north, some with haste, traveling day and night. A tagged sei whale once covered 2,100 nautical miles in ten days. Humpbacks swim to coastal Ecuador, nearly 4,000 miles one way. Right whales go only as far as Patagonia. They eat little if anything at this time and return to Antarctica the next austral summer with huge appetites, buoyant and still wrapped in blubber, their great hearts beating only eight times a minute.

"We observed a very great number of the largest-sized black whales," wrote James Clark Ross in Antarctica in December 1841, "so tame that they allowed the ship sometimes almost to touch them before they would get out of the way; so that any number of ships might procure a cargo of oil in a short time."

They were right whales, so called because they were the "right" ones to kill: coastal, slow-moving, complacent, the most peaceful of all whales, first to the slaughter in the northern seas. Their blubber yielded large volumes of lubricating and lamp oil; their baleen was fashioned into corset stays and umbrella ribs. Ross added, "Thus within ten days after leaving the Falkland Islands, we had discovered not only new land, but a valuable whale-fishery well worth the attention of our enterprising merchants, less than six hundred miles from one of our own possessions."

By the mid-1800s nearly a thousand whaling ships plied the oceans of the world, three-fourths of them American. In one 70-year period nearly 200,000 right whales were killed, most of them in the North Atlantic. Those stocks devastated, the whalers turned south. In 1849, only eight years after James Ross penned his prophecy, Charles Enderby, an English entrepre-

---

HUMPBACK WHALE SHOWS ITS FLUKES as it dives in Charlotte Bay, off the Antarctic Peninsula. The dives of most humpbacks last less than 15 minutes, as these whales typically feed on near-surface swarms of krill.

THREE KILLER WHALES, known also as orcas, spy hop in McMurdo Sound. Scientists theorize that killer whales do this to view the above-sea world and to search for prey. Orcas often travel in small family groups called pods.

neur with Ross's endorsement and a fancy for whaling, arrived in Antarctica. His venture proved unprofitable—a total failure, in fact, as sailors ended up scurvy-ridden, dead, or in the brig—but the idea of Antarctic whaling had been born and would not die. Reports from Ross and other explorers filled men's heads with dreams. In 1874 the research vessel *Challenger* recovered 60 ear bones of whales in a single haul while dredging the ocean floor.

While America plundered herself in the Civil War, a Norwegian named Svend Foyn began to modernize whaling with steam-powered catcher boats and bow-mounted cannons that fired harpoons armed with hinged barbs for keeping hold of the whales and grenades in the harpoon heads for killing them. The dead whales were winched alongside the boats, injected with air by a hypodermic lance, flagged, and floated. Some were rafted together with other whales, like logs in a sawmill pond, and retrieved later. Many were notched in their flukes, each notch representing a buried harpoon, so the men with flensing knives wouldn't hit the harpoon or possibly detonate a dud grenade. This was hardly a Moby-Dick affair with hand-thrown harpoons, a peg-legged captain, and square-rigged canvas

FOLLOWING PAGES: A humpback whale spouts, not only exhaling when it surfaces but also inhaling. The air passes through the blowhole at a speed approaching a hundred miles an hour.

sails. Whaling in Antarctica was a cold, mechanized slaughter. Stations were built on South Georgia and on other Antarctic and subantarctic islands. Large pelagic factory ships were added to the fleets. The carnage accelerated and lasted for more than half a century, until the whales became too scarce to find.

The whaling stations are quiet and abandoned now; the whales, largely gone. Of the original 100,000 humpbacks in the Southern Hemisphere, an estimated 3,000 to 4,000 remain. Of the 400,000 antarctic fin whales, 2,000; of the 150,000 seis, only 1,500. Most dismal of all is the southern blue whale, the largest animal on earth, reduced from 180,000 to 660, perhaps too few for the widely dispersed survivors to find each other, mate, and maintain viable populations.

Into the 1970s the Soviets hunted pelagic sperm whales for lubricating oil for turbine-powered aircraft, but they stopped when a replacement oil was found in the jojoba bean of the American Southwest. In 1985 the International Whaling Commission declared a moratorium on all commercial whaling in Antarctica. Japan objected and continued to kill minke whales for "scientific research," despite increased criticism after whale meat of several species was found in dinner bowls in Tokyo restaurants.

Large baleen whales are not abundant in Antarctica anymore; their scarcity is everywhere. Their white bones lie on windswept beaches, the tall vertebrae and long ribs under a patina of summer algae and winter snow. Penguins and seals come ashore and conduct their daily affairs. On South Georgia, elephant seals trumpet and joust in abandoned whaling stations, their voices strangely acoustic amid the metal and wood.

Visitors can feel a deep sense of loss here but also a profound sense of hope. The whales did survive; the seals, too. The great southern oceans harbor them. Penguins still scurry into the surf by the thousands, late for dinner, and return to their nests full of passion and krill. Their futures can be our redemption. "In a world older and more complex than ours," wrote naturalist Henry Beston, "they move more finished and complete, gifted with extensions of senses we have lost or never yet attained, living by voices we shall never hear. They are not brethren, they are not underlings; they are other nations caught with ourselves in the net of life and time, fellow prisoners of the splendor and travail of the earth." ∎

CHAPTER FOUR

On Thin Ice
Contemporary Research, Adventure, and Tourism

"I am trying to remember what I thought about Antarctica before I came here," wrote then Senator Al Gore in *The New Republic* in 1988. "For the most part I didn't think about it at all. It is just plain remote. From the other side of the world, in Christchurch, New Zealand, it is another eight hours due south by plane to the main U.S. base, McMurdo, and then another three hours from there to the South Pole." Stepping from the plane at the pole, Gore was stunned by the cold thin air, the blue sky, the bright sun. "Yet all that light creates virtually no surface heat," he observed, "because most of it is reflected right back into space."

That cross fire of whiteness attracts intrepid hearts now as it always has: some who wish to conquer Antarctica; others who wish to conquer themselves; many who feed on mystery, challenge, or knowledge—perhaps all three, even a dash of danger.

"We were sailing a sea across which none had hitherto

STEADY AS SHE GOES, the tourist expedition vessel *Mulchonov* plies through loose pack ice at nightfall off the Antarctic Peninsula. A strong bow light, shining from above the bridge, illuminates the route.

voyaged," wrote Otto Nordenskjöld, a Swedish geologist who traveled to Antarctica in 1901. Looking for fossils, he nearly became one himself. "The weather had changed as if by magic; it seemed as though the Antarctic world repented of the inhospitable way in which it had received us the previous day, or maybe, it merely wished to entice us deeper into its interior in order the more surely to annihilate us. At all events, we pressed onward, seized by that almost feverish eagerness which can only be felt by an explorer who stands upon a threshold of the great unknown."

In the latter part of this first century of human presence in Antarctica, everyone is still an explorer. Just getting there and back feels risky, despite traveling on ships and planes with computers and satellite-aided technologies. Force 10 gales still throw dinner plates across the galley. People still freeze to death. Everybody, scientist and tourist alike, still arrives with a sense of mission—and departs with a sense of accomplishment.

"I came here," wrote Senator Gore, "because Antarctica is the frontier of the global ecological crisis."

Antarctica used to imperil those who visited it. Now we, the industrialized human race, have imperiled it. A worrisome hole has opened in the protective ozone layer high in the southern atmosphere, leaking harmful ultraviolet radiation. Greenhouse gases have increased. Global warming may be under way. Certain ice shelves on the Antarctic Peninsula are starting to collapse, unprecedented since monitoring began. Some experts believe that Antarctica is in an early stage of accelerated melting. If global temperatures continue to rise, the melting may reach a point of no return.

One hundred years ago Antarctica had few human visitors and no permanent or temporary residents. Now it has about 15,000 scientists, support staff, visiting tourists, and shipboard crew who come each year, most in summer. The winter population is a little more than 1,000. More than 35 permanent scientific stations, and about 50 temporary ones, encircle and punctuate the continent and fly the flags of their host countries. Many are small biological laboratories or weather stations. The largest by far, the U.S. McMurdo Station on Ross Island, has been described as a small city.

Planes, helicopters, tides of tourists in red parkas, bundles of crushed aluminum cans, rusted barrels, and dedicated scientists with their computer models, VHF radios, down-link satellite telephones, and internet access—all create a modern counterpoint to wild, timeless Antarctica: a silent quartet of penguins, a Weddell seal under sea ice, a patina of lichen, the aurora australis in the infinite winter sky. The wooden huts built by Scott, Shackleton, and Mawson stand silent in the cold dry air, undisturbed and strangely evocative, as if the men had departed not long ago and would return soon, weary but victorious, full of stories and good cheer. They too are a counterpoint, instruments and relics of change.

At the South Pole, where the fates of Roald Amundsen and Robert Falcon Scott would converge in 1911 and 1912, a futuristic aluminum geodesic dome, 165 feet wide, houses a semi-subnivean science community at the U.S. Amundsen-Scott Station. Most staff and visitors arrive at the station by plane (U.S. Navy LC-130 Hercules on skis), as Senator Gore did, and enter a tunnel with a sign above it: "United States Welcomes You to the South Pole." The Pole itself, not far away, is marked by a red-and-white "barber pole" with a mirrored ball on top and is surrounded by the flags of the treaty nations. About 100 people live and work at the Amundsen-Scott Station in summer; 20, in winter. Most undergo psychological testing before they arrive. "Romantic ideas don't make it here," said one station manager. "This is not a place to come to escape from something. It is a place to learn new lessons about yourself."

In a nearby warehouse, fuel bladders hold nearly a quarter million gallons of diesel. Under the dome, scientists design tests, log data, and plot trends in atmospheric physics and paleoclimatology. They monitor the pulse of a changing Antarctica. They analyze snow that contains 200 times more lead than it did in prehistoric times. They decipher ice cores that contain dust, ash, and radioactive elements—signatures of volcanic eruptions and nuclear nightmares with such names as "Pompeii," "Krakatoa," "Hiroshima," and "Chernobyl."

The U.S. Amundsen-Scott Station is actually about 835 feet northeast of the geographic South Pole, but getting closer, since the ice and the station on it drift poleward about 32 feet per year. By 2025, the station and Pole will have merged. One mile in the other direction, the first U.S. station built in interior Antarctica (for the International Geophysical Year of 1957-58) lies buried in snow, unmanned. Each year it drifts farther away from the Pole, moving on ice that many millennia from now—provided Antarctica doesn't melt—will squeeze through the Transantarctic Mountains and emerge on the Ross Ice Shelf.

When Rear Adm. George Dufek landed in a Navy plane at the South Pole in October 1956 and stepped onto the wind-blasted surface, he became the first man to stand there, and the eleventh overall, since Robert Falcon Scott in January 1912. "The bitter cold struck me in the face and chest as if I had walked into a heavy swinging door," Dufek wrote. The temperature was -58°F, 90 degrees below freezing. Dufek was in charge of Operation Deepfreeze II, which would establish the first permanent

UNDAUNTED BY POLAR CONDITIONS, a tourist remains on deck of the vessel *World Discoverer* during a summer snowstorm. By 1998 more than 10,000 tourists a year visited Antarctica, and the number is still rising rapidly.

station at the South Pole. His chief of science was Paul Siple, a protégé of Adm. Richard Byrd. In 1928 Siple, at age 19, had won a Boy Scouts of America contest to accompany Byrd to Antarctica. Like Byrd, Siple would make great contributions to Antarctic science. For one, he would devise the windchill index to illustrate increased heat loss in severe weather. That summer of 1956-57, 84 supply flights dropped 760 tons of building materials, food, and fuel at the Pole. And by March 1957, 18 men had constructed a station and settled down for the 182-day polar night, the first party to spend a winter at the South Pole. The station they built is the one now buried in snow and unmanned; the present Amundsen-Scott Station, with its geodesic dome, was built in the mid-1970s.

When spring arrived on September 18, 1957, the temperature of -102°F set a record for coldness. But Siple and a companion took the expedition's dog, Bravo, for a walk around the world. "Bravo was the first to reach the red flag that marked the Pole," Siple wrote. "In fact, he had already made three trips around the world before we arrived.... Not to be outdone... I also strolled around the world, at a 100-foot radius from the flag."

FOLLOWING PAGES: Icebergs tower over tourists traveling from ship to shore by small inflatable craft. Here in Curtiss Bay, brash—fragmented—ice makes the going slow.

The International Geophysical Year (IGY) of 1957-58 was chosen to coincide with predicted maximum sunspot activity, when data collected in glaciology, meteorology, and geomagnetism could be compared with data gathered in 1932-33 during a time of minimum sunspot activity. So successful was this cooperative effort that the International Council of Scientific Unions approved the creation of a Special Committee on Antarctic Research, SCAR. It became the Scientific Committee on Antarctic Research, later hailed as "one of the most effective international committees ever formed." From these beginnings came a treaty.

Born in 1959 and baptized by ratification in 1961, the Antarctic Treaty has been raised on a steady diet of cooperation and compromise, of international give-and-take. It has grown and reached adolescence, become a United Nations of sorts, flexed its muscle, achieved brilliance, and—according to some—suffered disappointment.

The treaty was the first multinational arms control agreement to be negotiated since the end of World War II. It specified that Antarctica and surrounding waters be used for peaceful purposes only, that scientists of different nations freely exchange their findings and be free to visit and inspect each other's facilities, that no military exercises or nuclear explosions or disposal of nuclear wastes occur, and that each country strive to deepen and broaden the treaty's objectives to preserve the living resources of Antarctica. Before the ink had dried, many nations, including the United States, had launched into a frenzy of station building.

Biologist David G. Campbell observed in *The Crystal Desert* that "scientific stations represent a de facto claim…to Antarctic territory. And the American base at the South Pole represents a tacit occupation of all the wedge-shaped territorial claims, except Norway's, that intersect there.

"By 1991, 39 nations had signed the Antarctic Treaty. However, it is an uneasy alliance. Only 25 countries have been given full 'consultative' status, meaning they are allowed to participate in the meetings that determine the fate of Antarctica, conduct inspections of other bases, and modify the treaty. According to treaty rules, consultative membership requires a demonstrable research presence in Antarctica. This explains the plethora of new 'research' stations in the remaining ice-free areas…an ironic by-product…that has caused Antarctica more harm than protection." The

FIFTY-KNOT WINDS cut short a shore excursion for tourists. As this inflatable boat was being hoisted back onto the ship, the lines broke, and the expedition leader was thrown into the sea. He was rescued in five harrowing minutes.

first formal claim to Antarctic territory had come from Great Britain in 1908 and was so carelessly charted that it included parts of South America. Insulted, Argentina responded with a counterclaim that overlapped Britain's. Britain reframed its original claim to exclude South America but stridently retained the Falkland Islands, South Orkney Islands, and South Georgia, citing its discovery by Capt. James Cook in 1775. Thus, the groundwork was laid for sovereignty disputes that festered for more than 70 years and ultimately erupted into the Falklands War of 1982.

By the mid-1940s, seven nations—Argentina, Australia, Chile, France, the United Kingdom, New Zealand, and Norway—had sliced up wedges and served themselves more than 80 percent of the continental pie. Norway's wedge didn't extend to the South Pole; South Africa also made a claim, a small one, of a few subantarctic islands. Most nations constructed small permanent stations on subantarctic islands and temporary ones on the mainland. In 1954 Australia built the first large station, Mawson, on the mainland. Soon to follow was the U.S on Ross Island, at McMurdo Sound, and at the South Pole in 1956-57. The former U.S.S.R. built its first station at Vostok, still the coldest and highest of all Antarctic stations, located at the Point of Relative Inaccessibility, the farthest point from all Antarctic coasts.

Geographers recognize three poles in Antarctica, not one. The first, the geographic South Pole (true south and the site of the U.S. Amundsen-Scott Station), marks the southern end of the earth's rotational axis. The second is the South Magnetic Pole, where lines of force converge from the earth's south magnetic field. Because of the molten core of the earth, this pole moves five to ten miles a year, and is now near France's Dumont d'Urville Station on the Adélie Coast. The third, the South Geomagnetic Pole, located near Vostok, is the theoretical southern axis of the earth's magnetic field, around which the geomagnetic pole moves over millennia.

While treaty nations have agreed to hold their claims in abeyance, some employ thinly veiled schemes to augment their territorial desires. Argentina shipped pregnant women to their Esperanza and Marambio stations, where between 1978 and 1983 they gave birth to five boys and three girls, whom Argentina called "Antarctica's first natives." Chilean archaeologists then unearthed two projectile points in Escurra Inlet, on King George Island, in the South Shetlands, that bore a remarkable resemblance to quartz artifacts used by Indians in central Chile before 1500. "Their discovery was greeted with skepticism," observed David G. Campbell. "Was this a ploy by Chile…to push back the antiquity of its claim to pre-Colombian times?"

All this time, while the industrialized nations pumped chemicals into the air, a hole opened in the southern sky. Fishermen in Patagonia caught blind fish. Three-fourths of the elderly people in Queensland, Australia, developed skin cancer. Children were told the sun was dangerous; local laws required them to wear broad-brimmed hats and scarves for protection. Human immune systems weakened; cataracts increased. Was sunlight, a source of energy and life, becoming a harbinger of death?

The cause of the problem was not obvious. But in 1970 Paul Crutzen, a Dutch scientist at the Max Planck Institute for Chemistry in Germany, showed that ozone could be destroyed by nitrogen oxides. Then Sherwood Rowland and Mario Molina, both chemists at the University of California, Irvine, announced in 1974 that our atmosphere was being chlorinated by a popular family of industrial compounds called chlorofluorocarbons (CFCs)—more destructive than nitrogen oxides and commonly used in aerosol sprays, refrigerator coolants, and as foaming agents in polyurethane. The news was hardly welcome.

"Rowland suffered a form of scientific persecution," wrote Senator Gore in his best-selling book, *Earth in the Balance.* "Suddenly he was no longer invited to address as many scientific meetings; in at least two cases, companies profiting from the suspect chemicals threatened to withhold funding for conferences if Rowland was on the program."

Like Rachel Carson, who had authored *Silent Spring* 12 years earlier,

WILDLIFE VIEWING proves to be an absorbing pastime on South Georgia, where these tourists admire a bellowing southern elephant seal among a nesting colony of king penguins at Salisbury Plain (opposite).

Rowland stood by his beliefs in the face of daunting criticism.

Hailed as nontoxic wonder compounds, CFCs had sailed into American consumerism. They're inert, manufacturers said. What harm could they do? Science writer Jonathan Weiner explained in his 1990 book, *The Next One Hundred Years*: "In effect, these chemicals are the plastics of the atmosphere. They are inert. Nothing hurts them. They last and last. Rowland and Molina realized that such sturdy molecules would diffuse through the atmosphere until they reached the stratosphere. There, ultraviolet radiation would do what nothing on the ground could do: break them apart."

The liberated chlorine, acting as a catalyst, would bump into an ozone molecule and break it apart. Ozone (O_3), a simple molecule composed of three oxygen atoms, is similar to the oxygen (O_2) we breathe but has vastly different properties. Ozone is a pollutant at ground level with a distinct odor. In the stratosphere, however, 10 to 30 miles above the earth, it shields life below from a daily flood of harmful ultraviolet radiation. Rowland and Molina theorized that after the chlorine broke up one ozone molecule, it would wander off and break up a second, a third, a fourth, hundreds, thousands, and not finish until it met a nitrogen molecule and was neutralized.

Was this theory valid? Or was it Chicken Little? The sky falling? Each year during the early 1970s, industrial nations released a million tons of

SCIENTISTS MEASURE the 10- to 11-foot wingspan of an adult male wandering albatross. As they age, male wanderers become more white until they reach the "snowy" stage and turn completely white, except for wingtips and tail.

ADVENTURERS GO BY SEA OR LAND at the bottom of the world. Some sail past phantasmagoric icebergs. Others (opposite) descend by rope into an ice cave at 12,000 feet on Mount Erebus, the southernmost volcano in the world.

chlorofluorocarbons into the air. Rowland told a reporter, "I just came home one night and told my wife, 'The work is going very well, but it looks like the end of the world.'" Scientific journals offered conflicting summaries, as did the press. But evidence of thinning ozone did indeed grow.

In 1978 the Environmental Protection Agency (EPA) and the Food and Drug Administration (FDA) banned CFCs in spray cans. Then Ronald Reagan became President, and his director of the EPA, Ann Burford, wrote in her memoir, "Remember a few years back when the big news was fluorocarbons that supposedly threatened the ozone layer?" Secretary of the Interior Donald Hodel, also a Reagan appointee, said that if people are worried about the ozone hole, they should wear big hats and stand in the shade. When Al Gore ran for President in 1987 and spoke openly about the dangers of ozone thinning and global warming, columnist George Will described his candidacy as being motivated by "a consuming interest in issues that are, in the eyes of the electorate, not even peripheral."

"Rowland continued to predict a global disaster," wrote Weiner. "According to his calculations it would be a *gradual* disaster...."

"Lawyers for DuPont, the world's largest manufacturer of chlorofluorocarbons, argued in congressional hearings that it would be folly to kill their product on the basis of such far-off possibilities."

Meanwhile, far to the south, at a remote research station in Halley Bay, near the Weddell Sea, Joseph Farman, team leader of the British Antarctic Survey, wondered if he was going crazy. Ever since the IGY in 1957-58, Farman had measured ozone in the upper atmosphere, using spectrometers, which determine the chemical composition of a substance by the passage of light through it. In the spring of 1981, he noticed a thinning of ozone over Antarctica. He carefully checked his records and realized that a decline had in fact been happening for many years, always in the spring, but so slight it was nearly imperceptible. And each summer it disappeared. Didn't anybody else see this? "After the discovery in Halley Bay," wrote Weiner, "Farman scanned journals and technical research reports month after month, looking for independent confirmation of the hole in the sky.... The Antarctic team was under enormous pressure. The loneliness of the discovery matched the loneliness of the place."

By the spring of 1984, the ozone hole covered most of Antarctica and extended nearly to the southern tip of Argentina. A second British team confirmed its existence, and Farman published his findings. Three years later, when the hole grew to the size of the United States and Mexico combined, most atmospheric scientists agreed: We have a planetary emergency. That same year, 1987, representatives of many nations signed the Montreal Protocol, negotiated by the United Nations, calling for a worldwide CFC reduction of 50 percent by the year 2000. (CFCs had been increasing by 3 percent per year.) Many manufacturers, including DuPont, endorsed the plan. Nevertheless, in 1988 the world manufactured more than a billion pounds of CFCs. The hole worsened in 1989, and the agreement was amended in London in 1990 to state that the production of CFCs (and halons) must cease entirely by the year 2000.

"You mean you still believe that there is harm from this little *pssst, pssst, pssst...?*" a French minister once asked, imitating an aerosol can as he shrugged with indifference. "Yes," answered a growing chorus, orchestrated by the likes of Susan Solomon. Born one year before the IGY, and not even 30 when she first heard of Farman's findings, Solomon would become one of the best atmospheric chemists in the world. When questioned about her youthful appearance at conferences, she responded, "Age gets to be less of a problem every year." She led the first National Ozone

Expedition to Antarctica, where she confirmed Rowland's hypothesis. Then, with other chemists, she constructed a genesis of the annual ozone hole, why it occurs over Antarctica, and why in the austral spring.

Several reasons. First, winter air over Antarctica is the coldest on earth, especially upon the advent of spring, after six long months of darkness. Clouds of nitric acid and ice particles form in the stratosphere and enhance the abilities of chlorine to destroy ozone. Second, a strong circular wind—a polar vortex—holds the chemicals in place like a witches' brew in a bowl, waiting for the sun to return. Third, when sunlight strikes the brew, it triggers a chain reaction of ozone destruction, and the hole forms, often deeper and larger each spring. As the air warms up, the bowl loses its integrity. Surrounding air, which contains ozone, then spills into the area from the north and replenishes lost ozone over Antarctica but causes a thinning elsewhere. The hole heals, but "bubbles" of the ozone hole can break away, drift north over areas with large human populations, and pose serious health risks.

Unfiltered by ozone, ultraviolet light bombards Antarctica in two wavelengths that affect humans and other life: UV-A and UV-B. UV-B is the greater threat, not just to humans, but to all organisms. It depresses rates of photosynthesis in phytoplankton, alters chromosomal development and cellular metabolism, and could collapse—or contribute to a collapse of—the Antarctic marine ecosystem. Nobody is certain. The problem is unprecedented. But scientists do know this: When coupled with global warming, ozone depletion forms a feedback loop. Water vapor and greenhouse gases (methane and carbon dioxide) trap infrared radiation near the earth's surface, which warms the lower atmosphere and robs the upper atmosphere of heat. This accelerates ozone destruction, allowing more ultraviolet radiation to spill through a thinning ozone layer and strike the earth, a process that creates even more surface heat. CFCs are also greenhouse gases. One malady aggravates another. The upper atmosphere cools, the lower atmosphere warms, and the ozone decline worsens.

For more than a hundred years, since industrial smokestacks began belching into the sky black clouds of smoke from the burning of fossil fuels, scientists have portended global warming from the greenhouse effect: a radical increase of gases in the atmosphere that trap heat—gases put there by humankind. Antarctic ice cores (and atmospheric data from Mauna Loa, Hawaii) reveal a 25 percent increase in atmospheric carbon dioxide worldwide from before the industrial revolution to today.

Compounding the problem, tropical rain forests, the lungs of earth where carbon dioxide is absorbed, have been devastated by clear-cut logging and clearing for agriculture. And cold oceans, which absorb more carbon dioxide than all rain forests combined, are warming and losing their ability to mitigate the greenhouse effect.

In Antarctica, the West Antarctic ice sheet, the world's only remain-

ing body of ice that sits on the ocean floor rather than floats, appears unstable. So do some ice shelves. The apron of pack ice that surrounds the continent each winter, effectively doubling its size, is also vulnerable. Algae develop along this ice/water interface and sustain larval krill during winter, which in turn sustain penguins. Because there is now less ice along the Antarctic Peninsula, where temperatures have risen four to five degrees during the past 50 years, all three—algae, krill, and penguins, especially Adélie penguins—are in steep decline there.

Is Antarctica dying? Can it be saved? Or have we learned too little, too late? An environmental organization, Greenpeace, established its own base on Ross Island in 1987, the same year as the Montreal Protocol, and began questioning the policies of treaty nations that appeared more interested in protecting one another than protecting Antarctica.

In a report entitled "On Thin Ice," Paul Bogart, a Greenpeace Antarctica campaign coordinator asked, "…How will these countries police each other? Again, the past record is dismal. In the early 1980s, the French government began blasting a landing strip into the rocks at Point Geologie. The plan was an environmental disaster—the Dumont d'Urville base lies in one of the richest ecosystems in all of Antarctica, and the construction not only killed penguins (violating a key provision of one of the treaty agreements), but the airstrip itself divided a nesting area in two, cutting off the access of an entire penguin colony to the sea. The response from the treaty nations was, in a word, muted. At the 1985 treaty meeting in Brussels, not one country was willing to insist that the issue be formally discussed. The unity of the attendees was paramount, suggested some delegates, and such a divisive issue dare not be raised."

Bogart listed many treaty transgressions, including one reported by a British biologist who visited an abandoned Australian station: "Tinned and bottled food, machine parts, building materials, chemicals (including more than 200 boxes of tinned caustic soda, spilling their contents into the snow), metal drums, flares, and even explosives were scattered over at least a square kilometer." In the waters off the U.S. station at McMurdo, divers reported "…PCB concentrations comparable to those found in the most polluted estuaries and bays in the United States. Open burning and the presence of discarded truck tires, batteries, and plastics are all violations

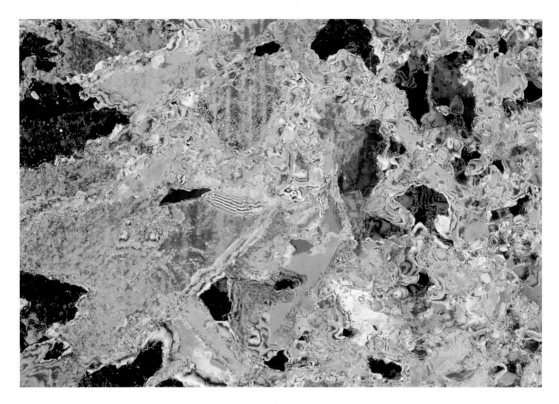

POLARIZED SIX-INCH cross section of ice core tells scientists how the ice formed, whether the seas it crystallized from were stormy or calm, and whether temperatures were cold or moderate. In addition pollen, volcanic ash, and radioactive particles help explain Antarctica's past and predict its future.

of the [Antarctic Treaty] Code of Conduct [for Waste Disposal]." When the U.S. experimented with a nuclear power plant at McMurdo, 1962–1972, and found it didn't work to expectations, it was removed from the base, along with 38,800 cubic feet of radioactive rock. Playing ruefully on Robert Falcon Scott's heartbreak at the South Pole, a poster on the wall at McMurdo read: "Great God—what an awful race."

By the late 1980s nearly every scientist and politician involved with Antarctica agreed that only international cooperation, not competition, would save the last continent. That spirit of cooperation was put into action on July 27, 1989, when an expedition of six men from six countries departed Seal Nunataks, on the Antarctic Peninsula, for the Soviet Mirnyy Station, on the Queen Mary Coast, 3,700 miles away. Their goal: cross Antarctica by its longest axis, using skis, three sleds, and 40 dogs. The cost: 11 million dollars. "We hoped our expedition would help focus the world's attention, and similar cooperation, on the icy continent," reported expedition coleader Will Steger in NATIONAL GEOGRAPHIC (November 1990).

"The next few years will be crucial to Antarctica's future. Increasingly it is beset by man-made pollutants.... Most important, the international treaty that governs Antarctica comes up for review...leaving open to discussion such vital issues as scientific research, mining, military presence, and territorial claims. As the world's greatest remaining wilderness, Antarctica's harsh yet surprisingly delicate environment must be preserved."

No doubt fresh in the minds of these six men was the wreck of the *Bahía Paraíso,* an Argentine supply and tourist ship that in January 1989 foundered on rocks next to the U.S. Palmer Station on the Antarctic Peninsula and spilled 170,000 gallons of jet and diesel fuel. Wildlife studies, 25 years in the making, collapsed. Just weeks later, the Peruvian research and supply ship *Humboldt* slammed into rocks near King George Island and left an oil slick nearly a mile long. As such disasters added to those of the ozone hole, global warming, and other growing threats to pristine Antarctica, peopled wondered: Is any place safe from humankind?

For 60 straight days the six-man expedition battled storms, crevasses, and katabatic winds on the crooked spine of the Antarctic Peninsula. Temperatures averaged -30°F. Each man consumed 6,000 calories a day to fight cold and exhaustion. Huddled in his tent, waiting, waiting, Steger reported: "Once in a rare while the wind would stop, abruptly and completely. Then, with an explosive bang, it was back; the guy lines whining, nylon slapping." Victor Boyarsky, the exuberant Russian, would climb from his tent in the morning wearing only booties, wash himself in the snow, then visit the others and shout in broken English through tent walls, "Mild today. Winds only 20 miles an hour. You'll need a face mask."

Geoff Somers, a member of the team and a veteran of the British Antarctic Survey, had flown to Antarctica the previous summer and stashed 12 large caches along the route. Each contained enough food for men and dogs for two weeks and was marked with a flag on a nine-foot pole. But now, on the peninsula in winter, two caches could not be found in the drifting snow. The men had to share their high-energy pemmican (dried meat and fat) with their dogs. In late September a resupply plane dropped desperately needed rations. A low point for Steger came in mid-October when a favorite sled dog, Tim, part wolf and only five years old, froze to death.

The expedition penetrated the Ellsworth Mountains and found kinder

SURROUNDED BY ELECTRONICS AND ICE, a ship's mate stands night duty on the bridge of the *Nathaniel B. Palmer* (left). The ship's spotlights glimmer off a large iceberg off the port bow. In the Crary Lab at McMurdo (right), a researcher examines the optic axis interference signal in a single ice crystal.

weather. "We had learned much from the early Antarctic explorers," wrote Steger, "lessons that now kept us alive.… Modern technology gave us an advantage but presented a danger too—allowing us to get so far from rescue that there was no such thing as retreat. Our only way out was forward. That's one thing we learned from Scott—to keep moving, no matter what.…

"Australian Douglas Mawson taught us to keep our eggs in separate baskets. In 1912 a sled carrying most of his food and equipment plunged down a deep crevasse, leaving him more than 300 miles and 50 days from camp with little protection. He survived, barely, but his two teammates perished. That's why we traveled with three sleds, each self-sufficient."

The international expedition reached the South Pole on December 11, stayed for three days of celebration and rest, then pushed on into the "area of inaccessibility," the most remote region of Antarctica, 800 miles wide and utterly lifeless. Elevations climbed to 11,400 feet. Thin air made every movement a task. Sastrugi, some six feet high, bucked the sleds like boats on a turbulent sea. Burning ultraviolet rays rendered the strongest sunblock lotions useless. The -20°F cold became more tolerable than the monotony of endless ice. Each man tried to remember the laughter of a lover, the smells of a forest, the taste of fruit.

As the six men braved the hostile nothingness, another expedition

NEAR RYVINGEN PEAK, a weak October sun rises over a camp of the Transglobe Expedition (1979-1982). At McMurdo, researchers release an ozone test balloon (opposite), as blue sky belies serious concerns about earth's ozone layer.

reached the South Pole on New Year's Eve. Reinhold Messner and Arved Fuchs had departed the inland edge of the Ronne Ice Shelf on November 13, 1989, in an attempt to be the first to ski across Antarctica, using no dogs, machines, or airdrops. Messner had been the first to reach the top of Mount Everest without bottled oxygen, with Peter Habeler in 1978. When he arrived on skis at the U.S. Amundsen-Scott Station, he commented, unimpressed: "Amundsen's ripped tent should stand at the South Pole, nothing else." Fuchs, if this journey succeeded, would be the first man to reach both Poles on foot in one year. Finally, on February 12, 1990, the two men skied into New Zealand's Scott Station on Ross Island, completing their journey of 1,550 miles in 92 days.

Meanwhile, the six-man international team reached Vostok on January 18, to become the first expedition to cross the area of inaccessibility on foot. Soon thereafter they hit their coldest windchill: -125°F. "You crawl out into these freezing temperatures and feel absolutely horrible," wrote Somers, who no doubt recalled an axiom written nearly 70 years earlier by his countryman, Apsley Cherry-Garrard: "Polar exploration is ...the cleanest and most isolated way of having a bad time...[ever] devised."

As they neared the end, they descended toward the coast through a belt of storms and reminded themselves: Be careful. Many alpinists die on the way down a mountain, not on the way up, too careless with their summit success. Two of the team had been lost in Antarctic storms before and

BLIZZARD CONDITIONS do not dissuade a researcher from checking instruments at Cape Davis, since waiting for good weather might take weeks. Men sometimes tether themselves to a hut so they can find their way back.

had nearly died. Qin Dahe, the team member from China, recalled a man who stepped outside to record weather data, became disoriented in a whiteout, and froze to death between two buildings only 160 feet apart.

And, in fact, only 16 miles from Mirnyy, the youngest member of the team, Keizo Funatso of Japan, stepped from his tent into a blinding blizzard to check his dogs—and disappeared. His teammates searched for him while tethered by a long rope to a sled, so they too would not be lost. They yelled into the storm: "Keizo…Keizo…!" No reply. Wrote Steger, "I envisioned the worst—carrying Keizo these last few miles wrapped in the flag of his homeland—and my stomach knotted in anguish." They searched into the night, waited out the dark, and resumed searching. Finally Keizo emerged after 13 hours, having heard their calls. "I am alive," he said, cold but unhurt. His teammates hugged him and cried.

Having become confused in the blowing snow, Keizo had realized his peril and done the right thing. With a pair of pliers, his only tool, he dug a shallow trench and curled into it like a sled dog. "Once I was in my snow ditch," he recalled later, "blowing snow covered me in five, ten seconds.… I could breathe through a cavity close to my body, but the snow was blowing inside my clothes, and I was getting wet. I knew my teammates would be looking for me. I believed I would be found…; I had to believe that.…

"In my snow ditch I truly felt Antarctica. With the snow and quiet covering me, I felt like I was in my mother's womb. I could hear my heart beat—*boom, boom, boom*—like a small baby's. My life seemed very small compared to nature, to Antarctica."

The next day, March 3, 1990, the storm abated and the team skied into Mirnyy. More than a hundred people greeted them. The six men had traveled 3,741 miles in 220 days and forged deep friendships. They had changed. So had the world: The Berlin Wall had crumbled; the Cold War would end. Nelson Mandela was free; apartheid would die. A note awaited them from Messner and Fuchs: "Congratulations on one of the great polar journeys of all time. Let us now fight for a 'World Park Antarctica.'"

"As we traveled home," wrote Steger, "we sensed a new awareness, a new curiosity, about Antarctica among people who turned out to greet us.… Perhaps our expedition—as a small example of multinational effort focused on the last great frontier—would be accepted as a contribution toward the world's new awakening."

Indeed, in 1991, the Protocol on Environmental Protection, appended to the Antarctic Treaty and ratified in January 1998, imposed a 50-year moratorium on all mining and oil drilling south of 60° S latitude. Research stations began to clean up. In 1994 the International Whaling Commission voted in favor of a Southern Ocean Whale Sanctuary, encompassing all waters south of 40° S latitude, which hold more than 90 percent of the world's great whales during parts of the year. "World Park Antarctica," an idea embraced for many years by the Antarctica Project, the Antarctic

FOLLOWING PAGES: Midnight light paints warm pastels on cold features of the LeMaire Channel, on the Danco Coast of the Antarctic Peninsula, a popular destination for tourists.

and Southern Ocean Coalition, Greenpeace, the Cousteau Society, and other conservation organizations, now appears attainable. Sherwood Rowland, Mario Molina, and Paul Crutzen won world recognition with the Nobel Prize for Chemistry in 1996. "If all goes well," predicted Rowland, "the ozone depletion observed in the past 20 years should be slowly reversed over many decades." That same year, one month before his reelection, President Clinton signed the Antarctic Science, Tourism, and Conservation Act of 1996, which was ratified into law in April 1997.

From its humble beginnings in 1965, when the first tour ship came to Antarctica, tourism now brings more than 10,000 people every year, a number that is expected to increase by 50 percent within the next six years. Most arrive on adventure/cruise ships and visit the same seal beaches and penguin nesting colonies on the Antarctic Peninsula and subantarctic islands. Some enterprising companies have leased decommissioned Soviet icebreakers to travel deep into the Weddell and Ross Seas (in the austral spring) to see emperor penguins. All visitors must comply with conservation measures set out by the Antarctic Treaty—and are briefed accordingly before they set foot on land. But as Jon Bowermaster reported in *Audubon* magazine, "Once on land, the inevitable gangs of red-coated polar explorers can't help but disrupt the unsuspecting natural communities.…"

Some scientists have criticized tourism in Antarctica, and some tourism officials (and tourists) have criticized science—to neither's benefit, as each builds its sainthood on the sins of the other. Returning home from Antarctica, tourists and scientists alike can be ambassadors. They can speak for the voiceless, search for solutions; they can tell the world that Antarctica is a barometer, that whatever befalls Antarctica will befall the world.

"This is no longer a time for inept platitudes about conquests and frontiers," says Antarctic veteran Colin Monteath. It is a time for new ways of thinking about our world and ourselves in it—what Al Gore calls "a new set of global goals." Only then will the ozone hole heal. Only then will emissions of greenhouse gases be reduced and controlled. Only then will rapacious fishermen stop plundering the southern oceans of fish, squid, and krill. "These are the last wild days…," says David G. Campbell. "Antarctica can no longer have an icy indifference to humans."

Neither can humans be indifferent to Antarctica. ■

Author's Note

A fascination with Antarctica has led
KIM HEACOX to travel to that continent nine
times. In addition, assignments have taken
him to Africa, the Galápagos, and the Arctic.
Heacox has authored and photographed four
books on Alaska: *Alaska Light, In Denali,
Iditarod Spirit,* and *Alaska's Inside Passage.*
He also conceived of and wrote the National
Geographic volume *Visions of a Wild America:
Pioneers of Preservation.* Twice the winner of
the Lowell Thomas Award for excellence in
travel journalism, Heacox writes feature
articles that have appeared in many national
magazines and opinion/editorials that have
been published through the *Los Angeles
Times/Washington Post* News Service.
He and his wife, Melanie, live in a small town
in Alaska with two sea kayaks, three guitars,
and one African drum.

Acknowledgments

The author acknowledges, with thanks, the
assistance of Henry Brecher; Nora Burkhart;
Tui de Roy; Diana Doerr, Clipper Cruise Lines,
and the officers and crew of the *World Discoverer;*
Nadia Eckhardt; Carmen and Conrad Field;
Gina Gowdy; Melanie Heacox; Mick Heacox;
Sara Hinsch; Brent Houston; Mark Jones;
Denise Landau; Frans Lanting; Kirk Newman;
Pete Oxford; Taylor Ricketts; Michel Sallaberry;
Doug and Kristin Siglin; Tony Soper; John
Splettstoesser; John Thiede; Heidi Turer; and
Walt Vennum.

The Book Division expesses its gratitude to the
many individuals, groups, and organizations
mentioned or quoted in this publication for their
help and guidance. We are especially grateful to
the following primary consultants: Alan Cutler,
Smithsonian Institution; Gary Fitzpatrick, Library
of Congress; and George E. Watson. In addition,
we also acknowledge the following individuals for
sharing with us their specialized knowledge:
David Bresnahan, Guy Guthridge, and John
Rand, National Science Foundation; John
Carlson, Montana State University; Beth Clark,
Antarctica Project; Ann Hawthorne; Bob
Hoffman, Marine Mammal Commission; Amy
Knowlton, New England Aquarium; David K.
Mattila, Center for Coastal Studies; Valerie
Mattingley; Clyde F. E. Roper, Smithsonian
Institution; Robin Ross, Marine Science Institute;
and Donald B. Siniss, University of Minnesota.

Additional Reading

The reader may wish to consult the *National
Geographic Index* for related articles and books.
The following sources may also be of interest:

Bickel, Lennard. *Mawson's Will: The Greatest
Survival Story Ever Written.* New York: Stein
and Day, 1977.

Campbell, David G. *The Crystal Desert.* Boston:
Houghton Mifflin, 1992.

Cherry-Garrard, Apsley. *The Worst Journey in the
World: Antarctic 1910-1913* (2 volumes). London:
Constable & Co, 1922.

Fogg, Prof. G. E. and David Smith. *The Explorations
of Antarctica: The Last Unspoilt Continent.* London:
Casssell, 1990.

Fothergill, Alastair. *A Natural History of the
Antarctic.* New York: Sterling Publishing Co, 1993.

Huntford, Roland. *The Last Place on Earth.* New
York: Atheneum, 1986.

Lansing, Alfred. *Endurance: Shackleton's Incredible
Voyage.* New York: Carroll & Graf, 1959.

Laws, Richard. *Antarctica: The Last Frontier.*
London: Boxtree, 1989.

Mickleburgh, Edwin. *Beyond the Frozen Sea: Visions
of Antarctic.* London: Bodley Head, 1987.

Naveen, Ron, Colin Monteath, et al. *Wild Ice:
Antarctic Journey.* Washington, D.C.: Smithsonian
Institution Press, 1990.

Sparks, John and Tony Soper. *Penguins.* New York:
Facts On File, 1987.

Watson, George E. *Birds of the Antarctic and Sub-
Antarctic.* Washington, D.C.: American Geophysical
Union, 1975.

Library of Congress Cataloging-in-Publication Data

Heacox, Kim.
    Antarctica : the last continent / by Kim Heacox.
      p. cm.
    Includes index.
    ISBN 0-7922-7061-4. —ISBN 0-7922-7065-7 (dlx)
    1. Antarctica. I. Title.
  G860.H356 1998   97-51932
  919.8'9—dc21   CIP

Composition for this book by the National Geographic Society
Book Division. Printed and bound by R. R. Donnelley & Sons,
Willard, Ohio. Color separations by Digital Color Image,
Pennsauken, New Jersey. Dust jacket printed by Miken, Inc.,
Cheektowaga, New York.

Visit the Society's Web site at **www.nationalgeographic.com.**

Photo Credits

Index

Pair of king penguins nuzzle in the snow.